STUDENT BOOK

WorldView 2

MICHAEL ROST

Simon le Maistre
Carina Lewis
Gillie Cunningham
Sue Mohamed
Helen Solórzano

Simon Greenall
Series Editor, British English edition

Longman

WorldView Student Book 2

Authorized adaptation from the United Kingdom edition entitled *Language to Go*, First Edition, published by Pearson Education Limited publishing under its Longman imprint.

American English adaptation published by Pearson Education, Inc. Copyright © 2005.

Pearson Education, 10 Bank Street, White Plains, NY 10606

Editorial director: Pamela Fishman
Project manager: Irene Frankel
Senior aquisitions editor: Virginia L. Blanford
Senior development editors: Karen Davy, Stella Reilly
Vice president, director of design and production: Rhea Banker
Executive managing editor: Linda Moser
Associate managing editor: Mike Kemper
Production editor: Michael Mone
Art director: Elizabeth Carlson
Vice president, director of international marketing: Bruno Paul
Senior manufacturing buyer: Edie Pullman
Text and cover design: Elizabeth Carlson
Photo research: Aerin Csigay
Text composition: Word and Image Design
Text font: 10.5/13pt Utopia and 10/12pt Frutiger Bold

ISBN: 0-13-184081-0

Library of Congress Control Number: 2003115897

Printed in the United States of America
2 3 4 5 6 7 8 9 10–BAM–09 08 07 06 05 04

Text Credits

Page 21 "River Deep, Mountain High." Jeff Barry, Ellie Greenwich and Phil Spector. © 1966, 1967 Trio Music Co., Inc., Mother Bertha Music, Inc. and Universal — Songs of Polygram International, Inc. (BMI). Copyrights renewed. All rights on behalf of Mother Bertha Music, Inc. administered by ABKCO Music, Inc. All rights reserved. Used by permission of Warner Bros. Publications. 59 "Wonderful Tonight." Words and Music by Eric Clapton. © 1977 by Eric Patrick Clapton. All rights in the U.S.A. Administered by Unichappell Music Inc. All rights reserved. Used by permission of Warner Bros. Publications. 97 "Matter Of Time." Written by David Hidalgo and Louis Perez. © 1984 Los Lobos Music (BMI)/Administered by BUG. All rights reserved. Used by permission. 135 "This Used To Be My Playground." Words and music by Madonna Ciccone and Shep Pettibone. © 1992 WB Music Corp., Webo Girl Publishing, Inc., Universal—MCA Music Publishing, a division of Universal Studios, Inc. and Shepsongs, Inc. All rights for Webo Girl Publishing, Inc. administered by WB Music Corp. All rights for Shepsongs, Inc. administered by Universal — MCA Music Publishing, a division of Universal Studios, Inc. All rights reserved. Used by permission of Warner Bros. Publications.

Illustration Credits

Steve Attoe, pp. 80, 104, 112, 116; Pierre Berthiaume, pp. 38, 57, 132, 138, 141; Kasia Charko, pp. 64, 67; François Escalmel, p. 31; Stephen Harris, pp. 63, 140, 142; Paul McCusker, pp. 18-19, 46-47, 85, 95; NSV Productions, pp. 83, 138, 141; Stephen Quinlan, pp. 33, 83, 95, 137, 139; Steve Schulman, p. 82.

Photo Credits

Page 3 *(top)* Doug Menuez/Getty Images, *(middle)* Cosmo Condina/Getty Images, *(bottom)* The Stock Market; 8 AbleStock/Index Stock Imagery; 10 Spencer Platt/Newsmakers/Getty Images; 11 *(top)* Aquarius Library, *(bottom)* Rex Features/SIPA; 12 Richard Smith/Corbis; 15 *(top right)* Stone/Stewart Cohen, *(middle left)* Stone/David Ball, *(middle right)* Pictor International, *(bottom left)* Ulli Seer/Getty Images, *(bottom right)* John W. Banagan/Getty Images; 16 *(top)* Peter Adams/Getty Images, *(bottom)* Stone/Lori Adamski Peek; 19 Arlene Sandler/SuperStock; 20 B.D.V./Corbis; 23 Ryan McVay/Getty Images; 26 *(top)* Graham Porter, *(middle)* Walter Hodges/Getty Images, *(bottom)* Getty Images; 27 Network Photographers; 28 Laurence Monneret/Getty Images; 30 *(left & right)* Ryan McVay/Getty Images; 31 *(left)* Amos Morgan/Getty Images, *(right)* Dorling Kindersley Media Library; 32 *(bottom)* Erik Dreyer/Getty Images; 34 *(A)* Danjaq/Eon/UA/The Kobal Collection, *(B)* Universal/The Kobal Collection/Bruce McBroom, *(C)* Moviestore Collection; 35 Moviestore Collection; 36 G.D.T./Getty Images; 39 Touchstone/The Kobal Collection; 40 Getty Images; 41 Tom Paiva/Getty Images; 44 *(A)* Hutchinson Library, *(B)* Science Photo Library, *(C)* Science Photo Library, *(D)* Corbis, *(E)* Science Photo Library, *(F)* Art Directors & Trip, *(G)* Katz Pictures; 48 *(top)* Getty Images, *(middle)* Getty Images, *(bottom)* Robert Harding Picture Library; 49 Getty Images; 50 Jose Luis Pelaez, Inc./Corbis; 52 Robert Harding Picture Library; 53 Getty Images; 54 Getty Images; 58 *(top)* Neal Preston/Corbis, *(left)* RubberBall Productions/Getty Images, *(middle)* Ryan McVay/Getty Images, *(right)* Digital Vision/Getty Images; 60 *(A)* Steve Cole/Getty Images, *(B)* Dorling Kindersley Media Library, *(C)* Barry Rosenthal/Getty Images, *(D)* Dorling Kindersley Media Library, *(E)* Getty Images, *(F)* Getty Images, *(G)* Liz McAulay/Dorling Kindersley Media Library, *(H)* Dorling Kindersley Media Library, *(I)* Stephen Oliver/Dorling Kindersley Media Library, *(J)* Steve Gorton/Dorling Kindersley Media Library; 62 Dorling Kindersley Media Library; 66 Adam Smith/Getty Images; 68 *(A)* Getty Images, *(B)* Corbis, *(C)* William R. Sallaz/Getty Images, *(D)* Getty Images, *(E)* Allsport, *(F)* Allsport; 70 Mark Adams/Getty Images; 72 Trevor Clifford, *(bottom)* Philippe Gelot/Telegraph Colour Library; 73 Trevor Clifford; 76 *(top)* Dorling Kindersley Media Library, *(bottom)* Dorling Kindersley Media Library; 77 *(top)* Getty Images, *(middle)* Richard Price/Getty Images, *(middle inset)* Getty Images, *(bottom)* Getty Images; 78 Stone/Zigy Kaluzny; 86 *(A)* Robert W. Ginn/PhotoEdit, *(B)* Daily Mail, *(C)* Bill Aron/PhotoEdit; 87 *(D)* Daily Mail, *(E)* Daily Mail, *(F)* Corbis, *(G)* Daily Mail; 88 Ryan McVay/Getty Images; 90 Pictorial Press; 91 Niall MacLeod/Corbis; 93 Mirisch-7 Arts/United Artists/Kobal Collection; 96 Philip Gould/Corbis; 98 *(top)* Redferns, *(middle)* Christine Cheney Putnam c/o ITA Hall of Fame Archives at the McCormack-Nagelsen Tennis Center in Williamsburg VA, *(bottom)* Corbis; 100 Dave King/Dorling Kindersley Media Library; 103 *(top)* The Image Bank/Barros & Barros, *(middle)* Stone/Kalvzny/Thatcher, *(bottom left)* Stone/Stewart Cohen, *(bottom right)* The Image Bank/Ghislain & Marie David de Lossy; 109 *(top left)* Mary Evans Picture Library, *(top right)* Hulton Deutsch, *(bottom left)* Hulton Deutsch, *(bottom right)* Topham Picturepoint; 110 *(A)* Richard Price/Telegraph Picture Library, *(D)* ActionPlus/Steve Bardens, *(E)* Stone/David Madison, *(F)* Popperfoto/Simon Bruty; 111 *(C)* Index Stock, *(G)* Robert Holland/Getty Images, *(H)* Allsport Concepts/Getty Images, *(I)* Murry Sill/Index Stock Imagery, *(J)* Getty Images; 113 ActionPlus/Steve Bardens; 114 *(top)* Rob Francis/Robert Harding World Imagery, *(bottom)* Corbis; 116 Camera Press, London (RING/RBO); 117 *(left)* EPS/Derek Santini, *(right)* Chika; 121 Jon Feingersh/Corbis; 126 Royalty-Free/Corbis; 128 *(top left)* Stone/John Beatty, *(top right)* Steve McAlister Productions/Getty Images, *(middle)* The Photographers Library, *(bottom left)* The Image Bank/Sparky, *(bottom middle)* Telegraph Colour Library/V.C.L., *(bottom right)* Britstock-IFA/West Stock Fotopic; 133 *(left)* RubberBall Productions/Getty Images, *(middle)* Michael Newman/PhotoEdit, *(right)* Getty Images; 134 Corbis, *(background)* Michael Matisse/Getty Images.

Introduction

Welcome to *WorldView*, a four-level English course for adults and young adults. *WorldView* builds fluency by exploring a wide range of compelling topics presented from an international perspective. A trademark two-page lesson design, with clear and attainable language goals, ensures that students feel a sense of accomplishment and increased self-confidence in every class.

WorldView's approach to language learning follows a simple and proven **MAP**:

- **M**otivate learning through stimulating content and achievable learning goals.
- **A**nchor language production with strong, focused language presentations.
- **P**ersonalize learning through engaging and communicative speaking activities.

Course components

- **Student Book with Student Audio CD**
  The Student Book contains 28, four-page units; seven Review Units (one after every four units); four World of Music Units (two in each half of the book); Information for Pair and Group Work; a Vocabulary list; and a Grammar Reference section.

  The Student Audio CD includes tracks for all pronunciation and listening exercises (or reading texts, in selected units) in the *Student Book*. The Student Audio CD can be used with the *Student Book* for self-study and coordinates with the *Workbook* listening and pronunciation exercises.

- For each activity in the *Student Book*, the interleaved **Teacher's Edition** provides step-by-step procedures and exercise answer keys as well as a wealth of teacher support: unit Warm-ups, Optional Activities, Extensions, Culture Notes, Background Information, Teaching Tips, Wrap-ups, and extensive Language Notes. In addition, the *Teacher's Edition* includes a course orientation guide, full audio scripts, and the *Workbook* answer key.

- **The Workbook** has 28 three-page units that correspond to each of the *Student Book* units. Used in conjunction with the Student Audio CD, the *Workbook* provides abundant review and practice activities for Vocabulary, Grammar, Listening, and Pronunciation, along with Self-Quizzes after every four units. A Learning Strategies section at the beginning of the *Workbook* helps students to be active learners.

- **The Class Audio Program** is available in either CD or cassette format and contains all the recorded material for in-class use.

- **The Teacher's Resource Book** (with **Testing Audio CD** and **TestGen Software**) has three sections of reproducible material: extra communication activities for in-class use, model writing passages for each *Student Book* writing assignment, and a complete testing program: seven quizzes and two tests, along with scoring guides and answer keys. Also included are Testing Audio CD for use with the quizzes and tests and an easy-to-use TestGen software CD for customizing the tests.

- For each level of the course, the ***WorldView* Video** presents seven, five-minute authentic video segments connected to *Student Book* topics. Notes to the Teacher are available in the Video package, and Student Activity Sheets can be downloaded from the ***WorldView* Companion Website**.

- **The *WorldView* Companion Website** (www.longman.com/worldview) provides a variety of teaching support, including Video Activity Sheets and supplemental reading material.

Unit contents

Each of the 28 units in *WorldView* has seven closely linked sections:

- **Getting started:** a communicative opening exercise that introduces target vocabulary
- **Listening/Reading:** a functional conversation or thematic passage that introduces target grammar
- **Grammar focus:** an exercise sequence that allows students to focus on the new grammar point and to solidify their learning
- **Pronunciation:** stress, rhythm, and intonation practice based on the target vocabulary and grammar
- **Speaking:** an interactive speaking task focused on student production of target vocabulary, grammar, and functional language
- **Writing:** a personalized writing activity that stimulates student production of target vocabulary and grammar
- **Conversation to go:** a concise reminder of the grammar functional language introduced in the unit

Course length

With its flexible format and course components, *WorldView* responds to a variety of course needs, and is suitable for 70 to 90 hours of classroom instruction. Each unit can be easily expanded by using bonus activities from the *Teacher's Edition*, reproducible activities available in the *Teacher's Resource Book*, linked lessons from the *WorldView* Video program, and supplementary reading assignments in the *WorldView* Companion Website.

The *WorldView Student Book* with Student Audio CD and the *Workbook* are also available in split editions.

Scope and Sequence

GRAMMAR FOCUS	PRONUNCIATION	SPEAKING	WRITING
Review and expansion: simple present and adverbs of frequency	Sentence rhythm/stress	Talking about how often you do things	Describe your weekend routines and activities
Linking words: *and, but, so*	Intonation in sentences	Apologizing and making excuses	Write email messages apologizing and giving excuses
Simple past: regular and irregular verbs	*-ed* simple past ending	Talking about past events	Describe an important time or event in your life
be going to for future	Stress in names of countries	Talking about plans	Write a letter to a friend about a trip you plan to take
Modals: *should* and *shouldn't* for advice	Weak and strong forms: *should, shouldn't*	Giving advice	Write an email giving advice to a friend on what he or she should or shouldn't do while visiting your country
Expressions for making suggestions	Intonation: focus words	Making suggestions	Write email messages giving suggestions and advice about parties
be and *have* with descriptions	Weak forms: *and, or*	Describing people	Describe the physical appearance of a friend, family member, or famous person
say and *tell*	Consonant clusters	Talking about movies	Write a movie review
would like/like, would prefer/prefer	Weak and strong forms: *would, wouldn't*	Ordering food and drinks in a restaurant	Write a memo describing the food and drink items for a menu
will for predicting	Word stress	Making predictions	Creating a web page about five predictions for the year 2100
have to/don't have to	Have to (*hafta*) and has to (*hasta*)	Describing jobs	Describe a typical day in your ideal job
Present perfect for indefinite past: *ever, never*	Linking vowel to vowel (*have you ever, has she ever*)	Talking about practical experience	Write a letter explaining why you should be on a reality TV show
Review: possessive *'s*, possessive adjectives/ possessive pronouns; *belong to*	Stress and linking in phrasal verbs	Talking about special possessions	Describe a keepsake that belongs to you or a family member
Adverbs of manner; comparative adverbs	Stressed syllables and /ə/ in adverbs	Describing actions	Write a short story or folktale

GRAMMAR FOCUS	PRONUNCIATION	SPEAKING	WRITING
Verbs for likes/dislikes + noun/verb + *-ing*	Stress to compare and contrast ideas	Talking about sports you like doing	Explain why you like or dislike a sport
Quantifiers + count/ non-count nouns	Vowel sounds: /u/ (*food*) and /ʊ/ (*cookies*)	Talking about what you eat	Explain which foods are good and bad to eat, and why
Modals: *have to/had to* for present and past necessity	Weak and strong forms: *to*	Talking about obligations	Write to an American friend about business practices in your country
Simple past and past continuous	Weak forms: *was* and *were*	Describing activities in the past	Describe a memorable event in your life
because, for, and infinitives of purpose	Stress in compound words	Giving reasons	Write an article about your favorite stores or restaurants and explain why you like to go there
a/an, the	*a, an, the* in connected speech	Talking about the theater	Summarize the story of the musical *West Side Story*
Present perfect: *how long/for/since*	Voiced and voiceless /ð/and /θ/	Talking about how long you have done something	Write an article that gives interesting facts about a person
Modals for requests and offers	Weak forms and blending: *can, could, should, would*	Making and responding to requests and offers	Write an email asking your job partner to do some tasks and offering to do others
used to/didn't use to	*used to/use to* (*useta*)	Talking about past customs	Compare your life when you were a child with your life now
Present perfect *vs.* simple past	Word stress	Talking about experiences	Describe your experience with adventure sports to complete an application
could and *be good at* for past ability	Weak and strong forms: *could* and *couldn't*	Talking about abilities in the past	Describe a sport or other activity that you could do in the past
Present perfect: *yet, already*	Contracted forms of *have* and *has*	Saying what you've done so far	Describe what you have already done and what you haven't done yet to reach a goal
Present factual conditional (*If* + simple present + simple present)	Vowel sounds: /ɪ/ (*give*) and /ɛ/ (*empty*)	Talking about consequences	Describe your behavior in a situation and explain why you behave that way
like + verb + *-ing*; *would like* + infinitive	The sound /ɚ/ (*work, earn*)	Talking about job and career preferences	Write a want ad for a job you would like to have

UNIT 1

It's the weekend!

Vocabulary Weekend activities
Grammar Simple present and adverbs of frequency
Speaking Talking about how often you do things

Lesson **A**

Getting started

1 **Look at the photos. What are the people doing?**

2 **Complete the sentences with the verb phrases in the boxes.**

go for a walk	~~go to the beach~~	go out for dinner

1. I love Sundays. I ___go to the beach___ on Sunday mornings. In the afternoon, I ____________ in the park. Then I sometimes ____________ with friends.

go to the gym	stay home	sleep late	watch TV

2. Saturday is my favorite day of the week. I ____________ on Saturday mornings. I like to exercise, so I ____________ in the afternoon. In the evenings, I ____________ with my family and we ____________ together.

get takeout	go to the movies	work late

3. It's Friday—almost the weekend! I ____________ on Friday nights because I want to finish my work before the weekend. I don't like to cook, so I ____________ on my way home. Then I ____________ with friends.

3 ***PAIRS.*** **Talk about the weekend activities in Exercise 2 that you like to do.**

I like to sleep late, go to the movies, and go out for dinner.

Listening

4 🎧 **Listen to the radio program about how people around the world spend their weekend. Find the photo that each speaker describes.**

Speaker 1 (Yuka) ____ Speaker 2 (Marcelo) ____

5 🎧 **Listen again and underline the correct information.**

1. Yuka never **gets takeout** / **cooks** on Fridays.
2. She often **meets friends** / **stays home**.
3. She usually **goes to the movies** / **watches TV** with her friends.
4. Marcelo always goes **to the gym** / **to the beach** on Sundays.
5. He sometimes goes out for **lunch** / **dinner**.

Pronunciation

6 🎧 **Listen to the rhythm in the sentences. Notice that the important words are pronounced longer, clearer, and stronger than the other words.**

I **nev**er **work** on **Sat**urday.
I **us**ually **go** to the **gym**.

What do you **do** on **Sun**day?
We **go** for a **walk** on the **beach**.

She **al**ways gets **take**out on **Fri**days.
She **goes** to the **mov**ies with her **friends**.

7 🎧 **Listen again and repeat.**

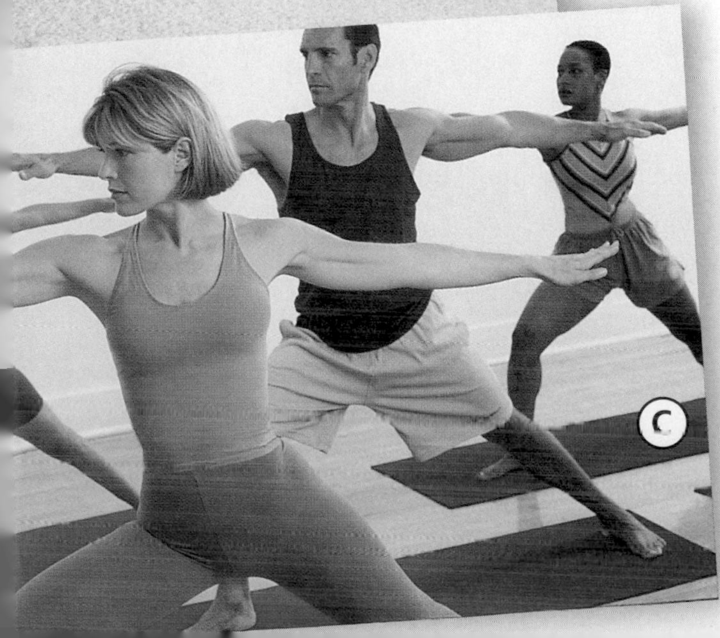

Grammar focus

1 **Write the adverbs of frequency in the correct place on the scale.**

always	never	often	~~sometimes~~	usually

100% ______________
____
____
sometimes
0% ______________

2 **Study the examples with adverbs of frequency.**

I **often work** late on Friday.
He **always goes** to the beach on the weekend.
The beach **is usually** crowded.

3 **Look at the examples again. Circle the correct words to complete the rules in the chart.**

Simple present and adverbs of frequency
The adverb of frequency comes **before / after** the verb *be*.
The adverb of frequency comes **before / after** all other verbs.

Grammar Reference page 143

4 **Complete the sentences with a verb and the adverb of frequency in parentheses.**

1. A: Her husband often works late on Fridays, doesn't he? (often)
   B: No, never. He ______________ to the movies with friends. (always)
2. A: What do you do on Saturday mornings?
   B: I ______________ to the gym. (usually)
3. A: Do you usually go out on Saturday night?
   B: No. I ______________ home. (usually)
4. A: How ______________ do you ______________ takeout for dinner? (often)
   B: I ______________ takeout on Saturdays. (sometimes)
5. A: I ______________ home on Sunday nights. Do you? (never)
   B: Yes. I ______________ a video at home. (sometimes)

5 *PAIRS.* **Practice the conversations in Exercise 4.**

Speaking

6 *BEFORE YOU SPEAK.* **Write five sentences about your weekend. Use each of the adverbs of frequency from Exercise 1.**

I never go to the gym on Sundays.

7 *GROUPS OF 3.* **Create a survey together. Each person, add one weekend activity to the survey form.**

How often do you...

Activity	always	usually	often	sometimes	never
go out for dinner?		✓			

8 *GROUPS OF 3.* **Take turns. Tell each other about your weekend activities. Use an adverb of frequency and give additional information. Check (✓) the box in the survey for each answer.**

I usually go out for dinner on the weekend. I usually have Italian food.

9 *GROUPS OF 3.* **Compare your weekends. Who has the most relaxing weekend? Who has the busiest weekend?**

Writing

10 **Imagine that your weekends are always perfect—you do only activities that you love. Write about your perfect weekends. What do you do? What don't you do? Use adverbs of frequency.**

CONVERSATION TO GO

A: How **often** do you work late?
B: **Never!**

UNIT 2

Excuses, excuses

Vocabulary Parts of the body; illnesses and injuries
Grammar Linking words: *and, but, so*
Speaking Apologizing and making excuses

Lesson **A**

Getting started

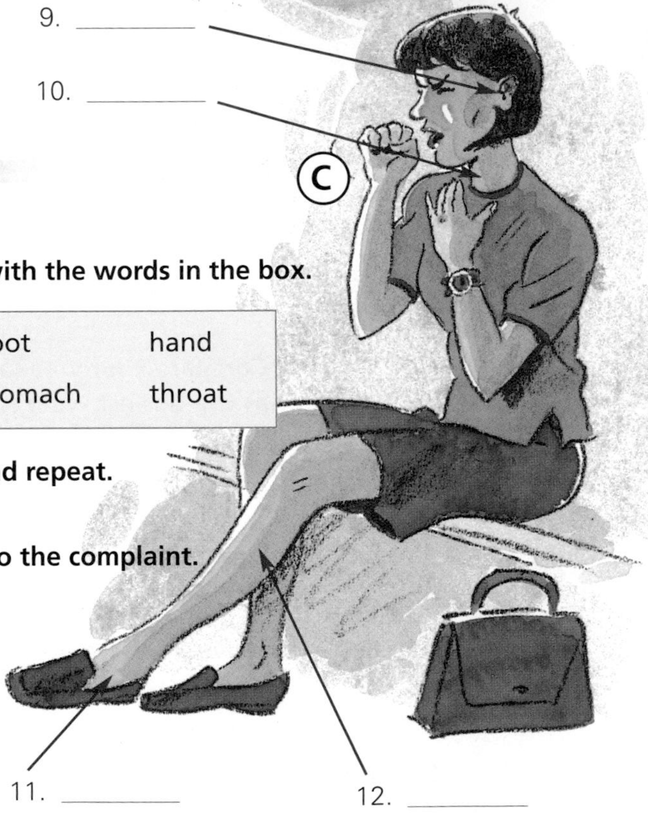

1 **Look at the pictures. Label the parts of the body with the words in the box.**

arm	back	ear	~~eye~~	foot	hand
head	leg	mouth	nose	stomach	throat

2 **Listen and check your answers. Then listen and repeat.**

3 **Write the letter of the person in the picture next to the complaint.**

1. "I have a headache." B
2. "I have a sore throat." ____
3. "My back is sore." ____
4. "I have a stomachache." ____
5. "I have a fever." ____
6. "I hurt my arm." ____
7. "I have a bad cold." ____
8. "I have a cough." ____

4 *PAIRS.* **Test your partner on the names of illnesses and injuries. Student A, point to a part of your body and act out the problem (for example, touch your throat). Student B, say the problem (for example: *Oh, you have a sore throat!*).**

Listening

5 🎧 **Listen to Tony tell his boss, Roger, why he can't come to work. Put his excuses in the correct order.**

____ He has a cough and a sore throat.

____ He hurt his back.

__1__ He has a fever.

____ He has a stomachache.

6 🎧 **What does Tony say to apologize? How does Roger respond? Listen again. Match Tony's apologies with Roger's responses.**

Apology	Sympathetic response
1. ____ I'm really sorry, but . . .	a. That's OK. Hope you get better soon.
2. ____ I'm afraid I can't . . .	b. That's too bad.
3. ____ I'm sorry, but . . .	c. That's OK. Don't worry.

7 *PAIRS.* **Take turns. Student A, use the ideas below and the complaints from Exercise 3 to apologize and make an excuse. Student B, give a sympathetic response.**

A: I'm sorry, but I can't come to work today. I have a fever.
B: That's OK. Hope you get better soon.

Apology

I'm afraid . . .	I can't play soccer today.
	I can't give my report today.
	I can't go out for dinner with you.
I'm sorry, but . . .	I can't come to work today.
	I can't help you lift that box.
	I can't sign my name on the check.
I'm really sorry, but . . .	I can't do my homework.

Grammar focus

1 **Study the examples with the linking words *and, but,* and *so*.**

> I have a bad cough, **and** my throat is very sore.
> I can't come in today, **but** I'll probably be there tomorrow.
> I have a fever, **so** I can't come to work today.

2 **Look at the examples again. Complete the rules in the chart with *and, but,* or *so*.**

Linking words: *and, but, so*
Use ___________ to add a similar idea.
Use ___________ to add a different idea.
Use ___________ to show the result of something.

Grammar Reference page 143

3 **Combine the sentences with the linking words in parentheses.**

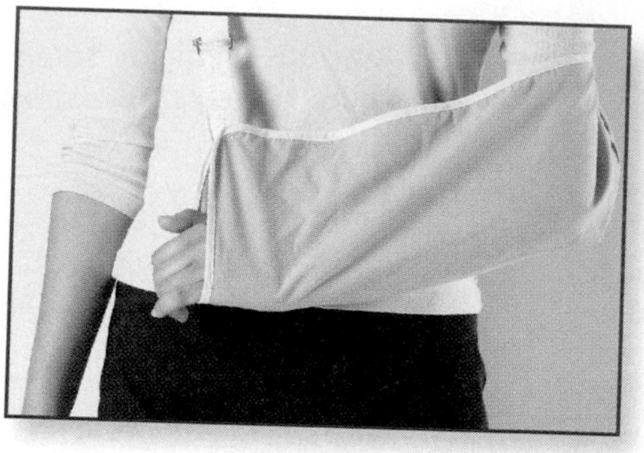

1. She hurt her arm. She can't use the computer. (so)
   She hurt her arm, so she can't use the computer.
2. I have a cough. I don't have a sore throat. (but)
3. My father hurt his back. My brother hurt his leg. (and)
4. I have a stomachache. I'm going to stay home. (so)
5. She doesn't have a fever. She feels sick. (but)
6. He has a headache. I gave him some aspirin. (so)

Pronunciation

4 **Listen. Notice the way the voice goes up on the most important word in each part of the sentence, and then down.**

I'm **sor**ry, but I have a **cold**.

I have a **cough**, and my **throat** is sore.

I'm really **sorry**, but I'm not **feel**ing very well.

I have a **fever**, so I can't come to **work**.

5 **Listen again and repeat.**

Speaking

6 *PAIRS.* **Take turns apologizing and making excuses using the expressions below. Student A, look at page 136. Student B, look at page 138.**

Apologize	**Show sympathy**
I'm (really) sorry, but . . .	That's OK.
I'm afraid . . .	Don't worry.
	That's too bad!

A: I'm afraid I can't come to work. I have a terrible headache.
B: That's too bad!

Writing

7 **You don't feel well today. Reply to each email message. Give an apology and an excuse.**

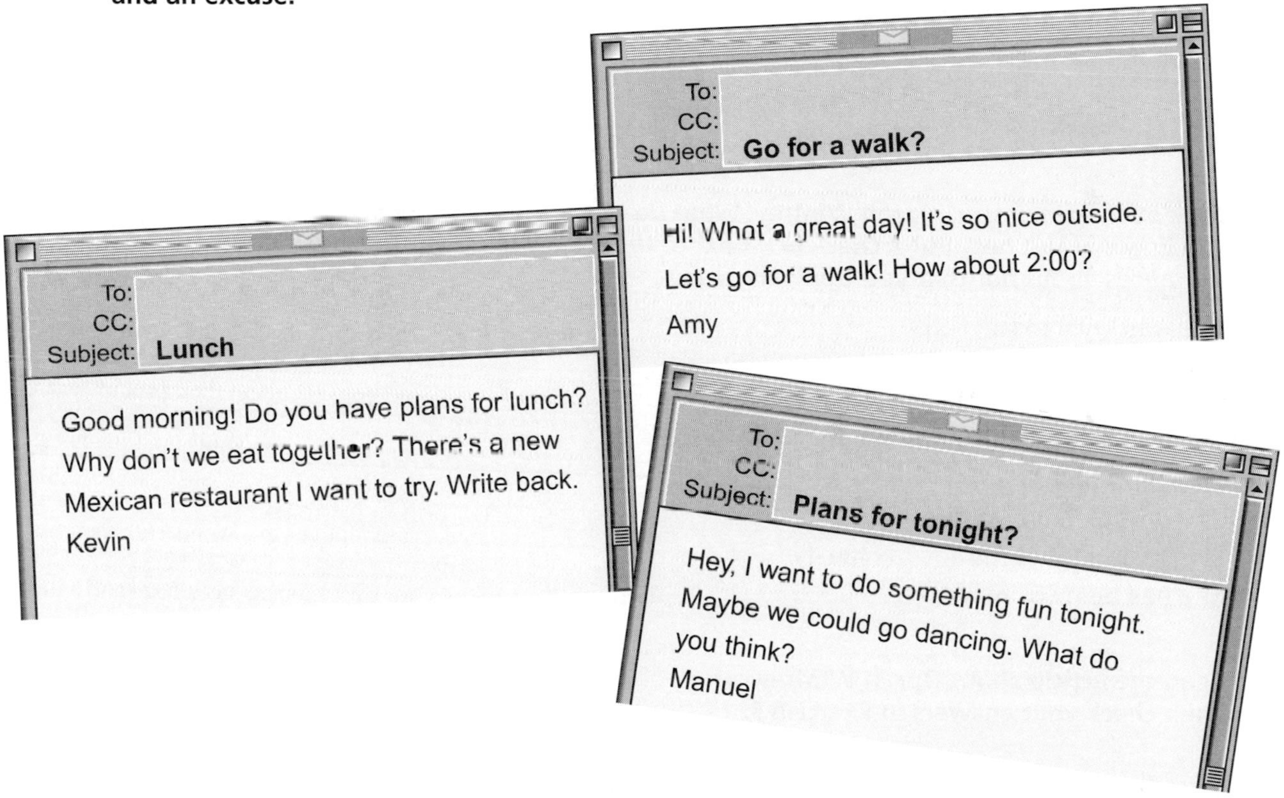

To:
CC:
Subject: Go for a walk?
Hi! What a great day! It's so nice outside.
Let's go for a walk! How about 2:00?
Amy
To:
CC:
Subject: Lunch
Good morning! Do you have plans for lunch?
Why don't we eat together? There's a new
Mexican restaurant I want to try. Write back.
Kevin
To:
CC:
Subject: Plans for tonight?
Hey, I want to do something fun tonight.
Maybe we could go dancing. What do
you think?
Manuel

Conversation to Go

A: **I'm afraid** I can't come to work. I have a sore throat, and I can't talk.
B: **That's too bad!**

UNIT 3

A life of achievement

Vocabulary Life events
Grammar Simple past: regular and irregular verbs
Speaking Talking about past events

Lesson A

Getting started

1 **Number the life events in the order they usually occur.**

have children ___	find a job ___	graduate from school ___
get married ___	grow up ___	go to school ___
work hard ___	be born 1	

2 *PAIRS.* **Compare your answers.**

Reading

3 **Look at the pictures of Oprah Winfrey. What do you know about her? Put a check (✓) next to the sentences about her that you think are true.**

She was born in the U.S.
She's an only child.
She's married.
She lives in an apartment in Chicago.
She has a plane.
She doesn't have children.
She gives a lot of money to charity.
She has her own magazine.

4 **Read the article about Oprah Winfrey. Then check your answers in Exercise 3.**

5 *PAIRS.* **Discuss. Did anything in the article surprise you?**

Oprah Winfrey

People in more than 132 countries watch *Oprah*. On this TV talk show, ordinary people talk about their problems and Oprah Winfrey helps them.

Oprah lives in a wonderful apartment in Chicago and has a farm and a house in the mountains. She has great cars and a plane too. But Oprah Winfrey was not always rich and famous.

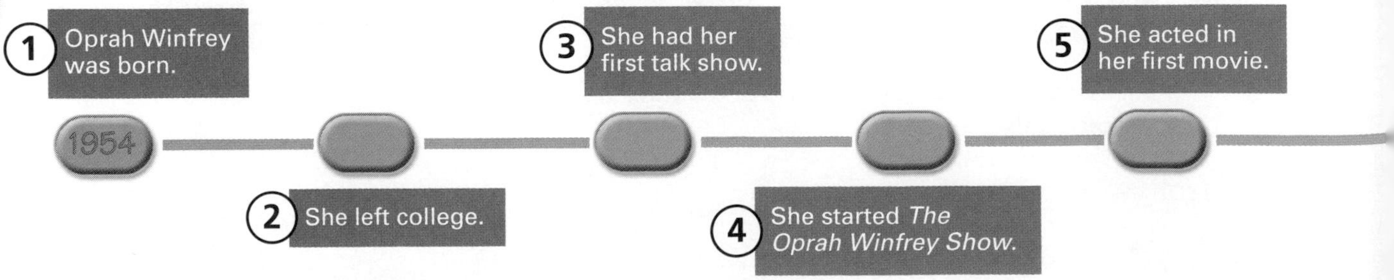
1 Oprah Winfrey was born.
1954
2 She left college.
3 She had her first talk show.
4 She started *The Oprah Winfrey Show*.
5 She acted in her first movie.

What kind of life did Oprah have as a child?
Oprah Winfrey was born in 1954 in Mississippi, in the U.S. Her family didn't have a lot of money. Oprah could read and write when she was three, and she loved books. She worked hard and was an excellent student at school, but she left college in 1973 when she was nineteen and didn't finish her education.

How did she start her successful career?
Oprah wanted to be famous, and her dream came true when she found a job in TV. She was the first woman and the first black newscaster on TV in Nashville, Tennessee. In 1977, she had her first TV talk show. In 1984, she moved to Chicago and started *The Oprah Winfrey Show*. It was a great success.

Oprah in *The Color Purple*

What did she do later?
In 1985, Oprah acted in Steven Spielberg's movie *The Color Purple*. After that, she made several other popular films. She didn't have any children, but she used her success to help other people's children. In 1997, she started a charity called Oprah's Angel Network. In the first five years, the charity collected more than $12 million and gave it to people in need. Oprah's Angel Network helps students to go to college, poor families to build their own homes, and communities to become safer. Oprah began her own magazine for women in the spring of 2000. It's simply called *O*. The magazine contains many personal stories and moving articles that reflect her interest in helping people worldwide. Her television program is still very popular, but now it's just called *Oprah*.

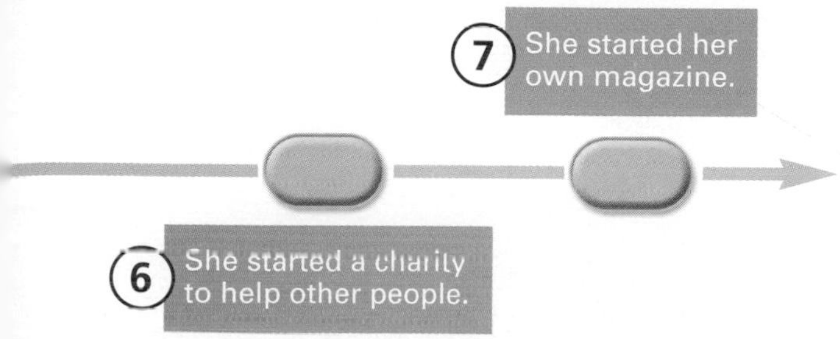
7 She started her own magazine.
6 She started a charity to help other people.

6 **Read the article again. Then write the correct years on the timeline.**

Grammar focus

1 **Study the examples of regular and irregular verbs in the simple past.**

Regular verbs Examples: *love, work, finish, end, want, move, act, start*	**Irregular verbs** Examples: *be, can, leave, find, do, give, have*
(?) How **did** she **start** her successful career? **(?) Did** she **start** acting right away? **(+)** She **started** *The Oprah Winfrey Show* in 1984. **(–)** She **didn't start** the Angel Network in 1984.	What kind of life **did** she **have** as a child? **Did** she **have** any brothers and sisters? She **had** her first talk show in 1977. Her family **didn't have** a lot of money.

2 **Look at the examples again. Is the rule in the chart true (*T*) or false (*F*)?**

Simple past: regular and irregular verbs
Use the simple past to talk about completed actions in the past. ______

Grammar Reference page 143

3 **Complete the story with the correct simple past form of the verbs in parentheses.**

The entrepreneur Anita Roddick __was__ (1. be) born in England in 1942. She ________ (2. open) the first Body Shop in 1976 in Brighton. She ________ (3. not have) experience running a cosmetic shop, but she ________ (4. have) a lot of good ideas. She ________ (5. want) to "make profits with principles." For example, she ________ (6. not allow) her cosmetics to be tested on animals. She ________ (7. pay) a fair salary to all her employees.

By 1993, Anita Roddick ________ (8. be) one of the five richest women in the world. But her principles still ________ (9. remain) important to her. In 2000, she ________ (10. leave) the world of business and ________ (11. become) a full-time campaigner on social issues.

Pronunciation

4 🎧 **Listen to the sentences. Notice the pronunciation of the simple past tense verbs. Check (✓) the verbs in which *-ed* is pronounced as an extra syllable.**

lived	wanted ✓	loved	studied	decided	worked
acted	finished	started	watched	used	collected

5 🎧 **Listen to the verbs in Exercise 4. Then listen and repeat.**

6 **Complete the rule.**

The *-ed* ending is pronounced as an extra syllable after the sounds ____ and ____.

Speaking

7 *BEFORE YOU SPEAK.* **Make a timeline of the important dates in your life. Include dates but no other information.**

8 *PAIRS.* **Look at your partner's timeline. Take turns. Ask questions to guess the missing information.**

A: Did you get a new job in 2003?
B: No, I met my fiancé in 2003.

9 **Tell the class something interesting about your partner.**

Sabrina met her fiancé in 2003.

Writing

10 **Oprah Winfrey encourages people to share their life stories on her TV show. What story can you share? Write a paragraph about an important time or event in your life. Use regular and irregular verbs in the simple past.**

Conversation to Go

A: When **did** you **finish** school?
B: In 2002. Then I **got** a job and **bought** a new car.

UNIT 4

Travel with English

Vocabulary Countries and continents; travel
Grammar *be going to* for future
Speaking Talking about plans

Lesson **A**

Getting started

1 **Write the countries under the continents. Then add two more countries under Africa, Europe, Asia, and North America.**

~~Australia~~	Canada	India	Ireland	South Africa

Australia	Africa	Europe	Asia	North America
Australia	________	________	________	________
	________	________	________	________
	________	________	________	________

Pronunciation

2 **Listen to the names of some countries and continents. Notice the number of syllables and the stress. Write each name in the correct stress group.**

O o	O o o	o O o
England	Italy	Korea

3 **Listen and check your answers. Listen again and repeat.**

4 *PAIRS.* **Test your partner. Say the name of a country. Your partner says the continent it's in.**

A: Australia.
B: Australia.

Reading

5 **Match the words to the photos on page 15. Write the name of the country.**

coast Australia countryside ________ market ________
safari ________ mountains ________

6 **Read the article. Then complete the chart.**

Country	When to visit	What to see and do
Canada	November	
Australia		Sightsee in Sydney Rent a car and drive up . . .
India		
South Africa		
Ireland		

THE TRAVEL WRITER'S

Dream Vacation

I have five months to travel before I write! I'm going to explore countries where I can practice speaking English. Where am I going to start?

Canada
It's the Rockies for me in November! There are mountains and beautiful lakes everywhere, so the views are great. I'd like to visit Nunavut, the home of the Inuit in the north of Canada, but unfortunately I'm not going to get there . . . there isn't enough time.

Australia
Australia is very hot from November to March. I love hot weather, so I'm going to arrive in Sydney in December. I'm going to sightsee in Sydney–there are so many interesting buildings in the city. Then I'm going to rent a car and drive up the coast.

India
Rajasthan is the perfect introduction to India with its festivals and monuments. There are also exciting markets to visit, with beautiful clothes and jewelry. I'm going to spend the month of January there. They say the weather is really nice then.

South Africa
South Africa offers luxury safaris and the chance to see wild animals. It also has a wonderful coastline, so, after the safari, I'm going to find a beach and go swimming there. I like the sun, so I'm going to go in February.

Ireland
In March I'm going to take part in the St. Patrick's Day festivities in Ireland. I know Ireland can be cold in the spring, but I'm going to buy a beautiful Irish sweater there. Dublin is a great city and the countryside is beautiful, so I think March is going to be a lot of fun.

Grammar focus

1 **Study the examples of *be going to* for the future.**

> (+) **I'm going to spend** a month in India.
> (–) She **isn't going to visit** the Inuit communities in Canada.
> (?) **Are** you **going to arrive** in December?
> (Yes, I **am**. / No, I**'m not**.)

2 **Look at the examples again. Complete the rule in the chart.**

be going to for future
Use a form of the verb ____ + *going to* + the base form of the verb to talk about future plans.

Grammar Reference page 143

3 **Complete the sentences with the correct form of *be going to* and the verbs in parentheses.**

1. She isn't going to travel **(not travel)** to Australia in July when the weather is cold.
2. She ______________ **(see)** beautiful monuments in India.
3. We ______________ **(walk)** by the lake in Canada.
4. They ______________ **(not stay)** in luxury hotels in India.
5. ______________ **(we / swim)** in the ocean in South Africa?
6. I ______________ **(visit)** Alice Springs and other famous places in Australia.
7. He ______________ **(take part)** in the St. Patrick's Day festivities in Ireland.
8. ______________ **(you / climb)** any mountains in Canada?
9. When ______________ **(he / leave)** Rio de Janeiro?

4 **Answer these questions about the travel writer in the article on page 15.**

1. What is the woman going to do for five months?
2. Is she going to visit Nunavut in Canada? Why?
3. When is she going to arrive in Sydney? Why?
4. What is she going to do in Rajasthan?
5. Where is she going to go in February? Why?
6. What is she going to buy in Ireland?

Speaking

5 *BEFORE YOU SPEAK.* **You're going to plan a group vacation to three countries where you can use your English. Look again at the article on page 15 and answer these questions. Write notes in the chart.**

1. Which three countries do you want to visit?
2. When do you want to go? Why?
3. What are you going to see and do?

Place	When to visit / Why?	What to see and do
Australia	May—it's cool then	Sightsee in Sydney . . .

6 *GROUPS OF 4.* **Take turns telling each other about your choices. Give reasons.**

I want to go to . . . in . . . because . . .

7 **Discuss your choices. Make a decision together. Where will you go? When will you go? What are you going to see and do there?**

8 **Tell the class your group's decisions. Can you agree on a class vacation?**

Writing

9 **Write a letter to a friend. Tell him or her about a trip you are planning. Where are you going to go? What are you going to do there? Use *be going to*.**

CONVERSATION TO GO

A: What **are** you **going to do** next summer?
B: **I'm going to fly** around the world.

Review 1 Units 1–4

Unit 1 It's the weekend!

1 Listen to the model conversation.

2 Walk around the room. Find someone who . . .

always goes to the gym on weekends. ______________
usually goes out to eat on weekends. ______________
sometimes goes to the movies on weekends. ______________
never sleeps late on weekends. ______________

3 *PAIRS.* Compare your answers. Did you find the same people?

Unit 2 Excuses, excuses

4 Listen to the model conversation.

5 *TWO PAIRS.* Play the Health Game. Take turns. Toss a coin (one side = move ahead one space, the other side = move ahead two spaces).

When you land on a space, look at the picture. Role-play a conversation between a boss and an employee. Student A, you're the employee. You can't go to work. Give an excuse using the situation in the picture. Student B, you're the boss. Respond to the excuse. The first team to reach FINISH wins.

Unit 3 A life of achievement

6 Listen to the model conversation.

7 Write three true statements about your past. Then write three statements that are not true but sound possible.

8 *GROUPS OF 3.* Take turns. Say one statement aloud. The others in the group guess "True" or "False." After everyone guesses, tell the truth! Players receive one point for each correct guess. The person with the most points is the winner.

Points: ________________

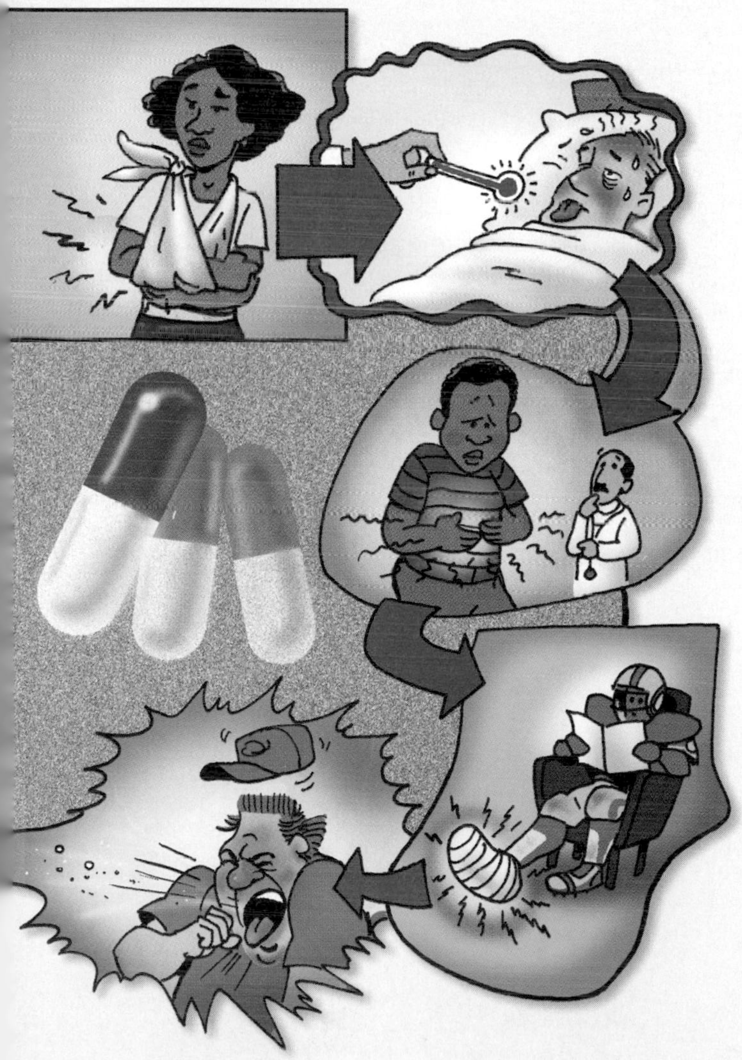

Unit 4 Travel with English

9 Listen to the model conversation.

10 *GROUPS OF 3.* Dario is going on a trip. Take turns. Ask questions to fill in his schedule. (Don't look at your partners' schedules.)

Student A, look at page 136.
Student B, look at page 138.
Student C, look at page 142.

11 *GROUPS OF 3.* Compare your schedules. Does everyone have the same information?

World of Music 1

River Deep, Mountain High

Ike and Tina Turner

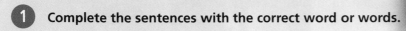

The 60s

***Tina Turner** was a teenager when she began singing with her husband Ike's band in the 60s. She went on to become an international superstar—and a symbol of the independent woman.*

Vocabulary

1 **Complete the sentences with the correct word or words.**

deep	faithful	flows	~~followed~~	goes on
let	lost	owned	puppy	robin

1. Tom's little sister always <u>followed</u> him around when they were kids.
2. Ines promised to help Ralph move, but she went dancing instead. She really ________ him down.
3. Yasuhiro is really upset because he ________ his keys.
4. They're excited about their new car. It's the first one they've ever ________.
5. The river ________ into the sea a few miles from here.
6. This isn't the last stop. The train ________ to Washington.
7. The children can't wait to get home from school so they can play with their ________.
8. You know it's spring when you see a ________.
9. A ________ friend is someone who is always there to help you.
10. Don't let the children play near the pool over there. The water is very ________.

Listening

2 **Listen to the song "River Deep, Mountain High." Correct the statements.**

1. The singer is singing about a love in the past.
2. The singer thinks that her love is getting weaker.
3. The singer will be as friendly as a puppy.

3 Listen to the song again. Complete the lyrics with the words you hear.

River Deep, Mountain High

When I was a little girl I had a rag doll;
The only doll I've ever owned.
Now I love you just the way I loved that rag doll;
But only now my love has grown.
And it gets ___________ in every way,
And it gets ___________ let me say,
And it gets ___________ day by day.

[Chorus]

Do I love you? My, oh, my!
River deep, mountain high
If I lost you, would I cry?
Oh, how I love you, baby, baby, baby, baby.

When you were a young boy did you have a puppy
that always followed you around?
Well, I'm gonna be as faithful as that puppy.
No, I'll never let you down.
'Cause it goes on and on like a river flows.
And it gets ___________, baby, and heaven knows,
And it gets ___________, baby, as it grows.

[Repeat chorus]

I love you, baby, like a flower loves the spring.
And I love you, baby, like a robin loves to sing.
And I love you, baby, like a schoolboy loves his pie.
And I love you, baby, river deep, mountain high.

[Repeat chorus]

4 *PAIRS.* **Compare your answers.**

Speaking

5 *PAIRS.* **In the song "River Deep, Mountain High," what are some words that the singer uses to talk about her love?**

6 *GROUPS OF 3.* **Discuss the questions.**

Do you like this song?
How does the song make you feel?

UNIT 5

Culture shock

Vocabulary Social etiquette
Grammar Modals: *should* and *shouldn't* for advice
Speaking Giving advice

Lesson A

Getting started

1 **Match the words and phrases in the box with the pictures. Some pictures have more than one description.**

1. give a gift _D_
2. use first names ____
3. take your shoes off ____
4. shake hands ____
5. kiss ____
6. wear a suit ____
7. bow ____
8. arrive on time ____

2 *PAIRS.* **Talk about the pictures.**

Which of these things do you do in your country?

A

B

C

D

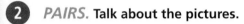

Listening

3 **Listen to a businesswoman give advice to her colleagues on living and working in the U.S. Number the topics in the order she talks about them.**

_1_ arriving for meetings

___ shaking hands

___ exchanging business cards

___ visiting someone's home

___ using a person's first or last name

___ deciding what clothing to wear

4 **Listen again and complete the statements about business etiquette in the U.S.**

1. For business appointments, always arrive _on time_.
2. The first thing people do at meetings is ________.
3. People usually exchange ________ at some point during a meeting.
4. If it's not clear what you should call a person, use his or her ________.
5. Take flowers or a ________ when you visit someone's home.
6. Don't ________ when you enter someone's home.
7. Wear ________ to formal business meetings.

Grammar focus

1 **Study the examples of *should* and *shouldn't* for advice.**

You **should arrive** on time.	You **shouldn't take** your shoes off.
Should we **bow**?	Yes, you **should**. / No, you **shouldn't**.

2 **Look at the examples again. Complete the rules in the chart.**

***should* and *shouldn't* for advice**
Use __________ + the base form of the verb to say that something is a good idea.
Use __________ + the base form of the verb to say that something is a bad idea.

Grammar Reference page 144

3 **Complete the sentences in the quiz with *should* or *shouldn't*.**

Culture Quiz

1 Should you talk about business at a meal in China?
a. Yes, you <u>should</u>. b. No, you shouldn't.

2 Should you wear a suit and tie to meet a new client in Saudi Arabia?
a. Yes, you should. b. No, you __________.

3 __________ you give a Brazilian purple flowers?
a. Yes, you __________. It's lucky.
b. No, you shouldn't. It's unlucky.

4 When someone gives you a gift in Japan, __________ you open it . . .
a. immediately? b. later?

5 In Mexico, __________ you shake hands with both men and women?
a. Yes, you should. b. No, you __________.

6 __________ you use your right hand or your left hand to accept a gift in Muslim countries?
a. right b. left

7 In the U.S., it is important to arrive on time. When you are invited to a friend's house, you __________ arrive more than 15 minutes late.
a. true b. false

8 You __________ touch a person on the head because it is not polite. This statement is true in which country?
a. Thailand b. Peru

9 You __________ have a meeting in Room 4 because it is unlucky. This statement is true in which country?
a. Mexico b. China

10 In Japan, you __________ use your boss's first name because it is not polite.
a. true b. false

Culture Quiz answers
1.b, 2.a, 3.b, 4.b, 5.a, 6.a, 7.a, 8.a, 9.b, 10.a

4 **Take the quiz. Then check your answers.**

Pronunciation

5 🎧 **Listen. Notice the weak and strong pronunciations of *should* and the strong pronunciation of *shouldn't*.**

You should arrive on time.	You **shouldn't** take your shoes off.
Should I take a gift?	Yes, you **should**.
Shouldn't I wear a suit?	No, you **shouldn't**.

6 🎧 **Listen again and repeat.**

7 🎧 **Listen and underline the word you hear.**

1. You **should** / **shouldn't** arrive early.
2. You **should** / **shouldn't** ask questions.
3. **Should** / **Shouldn't** I use first names?
4. You **should** / **shouldn't** take flowers.
5. **Should** / **Shouldn't** I shake hands with everyone?

Speaking

8 *BEFORE YOU SPEAK.* **Some friends from another country are going to visit your country. What should they do while visiting? What shouldn't they do? Write your ideas about the topics.**

Greeting/Saying hello
You should . . .
You shouldn't . . .
Giving gifts

Eating

Clothes

Other

9 *GROUPS OF 4.* **Compare the advice you're going to give your friends. What advice is the same? What advice is different?**

Writing

10 **Write an email to a friend who is going to visit your country. Give advice about what he or she should and shouldn't do during the trip.**

Conversation to Go

A: **Should** I bow when I meet someone?
B: No, you **shouldn't**. You **should** shake hands.

UNIT 6

Party time!

Vocabulary Planning parties
Grammar Expressions for making suggestions
Speaking Making suggestions

Lesson A

Getting started

1 *PAIRS.* **Look at the photos. In which photo can you see . . .**

1. a birthday party? ___
2. a costume party? ___
3. a going-away party? ___

2 *PAIRS.* **Discuss the questions.**

Do you like parties?

What is your favorite kind of party?

Have you ever been to a going-away party or a costume party?

How do you usually celebrate your birthday?

A

B

C

3 **Complete the pairs of sentences with words from the box.**

afford	buy	~~cost~~	pay	rent	spend

1. A birthday cake can __cost__ about $25.
   The gifts for Sue and Ron's going-away party __cost__ a lot.
2. I'm going to ________ a new dress for the party.
   I want to ________ a gift for you.
3. Can you ________ that suit? It's very expensive.
   I can't ________ a fancy restaurant. I don't have much money.
4. John is going to ________ for dinner on your birthday.
   He'll ________ by credit card.
5. I usually ________ a lot of money on birthday cards.
   We're going to ________ $300 on the party.
6. I want to ________ a car for the weekend.
   He's going to ________ a ballroom at a hotel for the party.

4 *PAIRS.* **Take turns saying three sentences about yourself or people you know. Use the verbs from Exercise 3.**

Listening

5 **Listen to a professional party planner talking with a client from an advertising company. They are discussing the company's yearly office party. Check (✓) the things they talk about.**

Party Planners, Etc.

- ○ *date of the party*
- ✓ *place*
- ○ *gifts*
- ○ *number of guests*
- ○ *music*
- ○ *food*
- ○ *parking*

6 **Listen again and underline the correct information.**

1. The party is going to be at **a hotel** / **the office**.
2. They're going to have **a band** / **a DJ**.
3. They're going to serve **dessert** / **dinner**.

Grammar focus

1 **Study the examples. Notice the ways to make suggestions.**

How about looking at how much we spent last year?
Why don't we rent the room at the Sheraton again?
Let's (not) have it at the office.
Maybe you **could** get a DJ this time.

2 **Look at the examples again. Complete the rules in the chart.**

Why don't/How about/Let's (not)/Maybe . . . could for suggestions
Use ______________ + verb + *-ing*.
Use ______________ + subject + *could* + the base form of the verb.
Use ______________ + subject + the base form of the verb.
Use ______________ + the base form of the verb.

Grammar Reference page 144

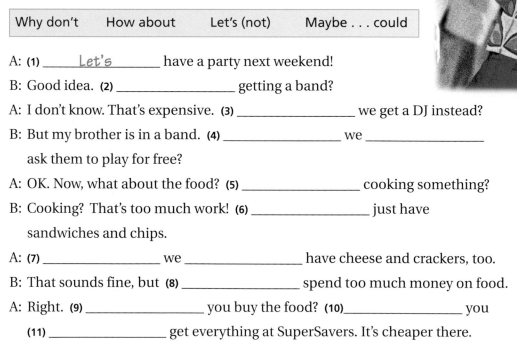

3 **Complete the conversation with the expressions in the box.**

Why don't	How about	Let's (not)	Maybe . . . could

A: **(1)** ___Let's___ have a party next weekend!
B: Good idea. **(2)** ______________ getting a band?
A: I don't know. That's expensive. **(3)** ______________ we get a DJ instead?
B: But my brother is in a band. **(4)** ______________ we ______________ ask them to play for free?
A: OK. Now, what about the food? **(5)** ______________ cooking something?
B: Cooking? That's too much work! **(6)** ______________ just have sandwiches and chips.
A: **(7)** ______________ we ______________ have cheese and crackers, too.
B: That sounds fine, but **(8)** ______________ spend too much money on food.
A: Right. **(9)** ______________ you buy the food? **(10)** ______________ you **(11)** ______________ get everything at SuperSavers. It's cheaper there.

Pronunciation

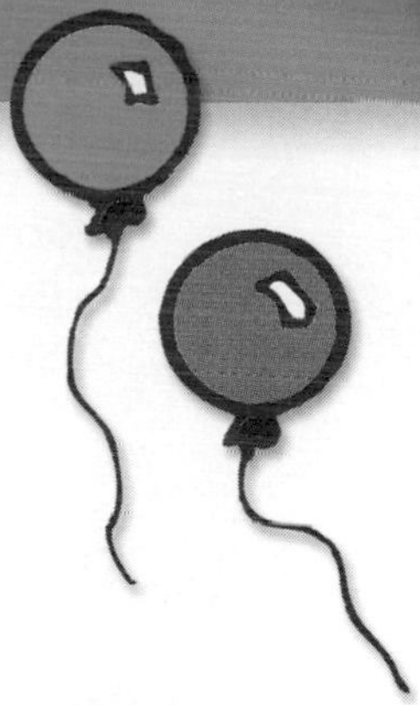

4 **Listen. Notice the way the focus word (the most important word) in each sentence stands out from the other words.**

A: Let's have a **par**ty next weekend.
B: Good i**de**a. Why don't we get a **band**?
A: We can't af**ford** it. How about getting a **DJ**?
B: **O**K. What about **food**?
A: Maybe we could order **piz**za.
B: I don't **like** pizza. Why don't we just have **snacks**?

5 **Listen again and repeat.**

Speaking

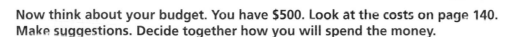

6 *GROUPS OF 4.* **Your group is going to work together to plan a party. First, choose the purpose of the party.**

- Surprise birthday party for (name)
- End-of-the-year party
- Other: ____________________

Now think about your budget. You have $500. Look at the costs on page 140. Make suggestions. Decide together how you will spend the money.

A: Let's have the party at a hotel.
B: Why don't we have it at the office? We can save $150.

7 **Tell the class about your group's party plans.**

Writing

8 **You are a party planner for a company called Parties Unlimited. People write to you for advice on giving parties. Read the email messages on page 136 and write replies to each one. Use *maybe you could, why don't you,* and *how about*.**

CONVERSATION TO GO

A: It's your birthday. **Let's** have a party!
B: I'd rather get a gift!

UNIT 7

First impressions

Vocabulary Words to describe physical appearance
Grammar *be* and *have* with descriptions
Speaking Describing people

Lesson A

Getting started

1 **Write the descriptions in the box next to the correct words in the word webs.**

average height	average weight	bald	beard	curly
elderly	heavy	middle-aged	mustache	short
sideburns	slim	straight	tall	~~young~~

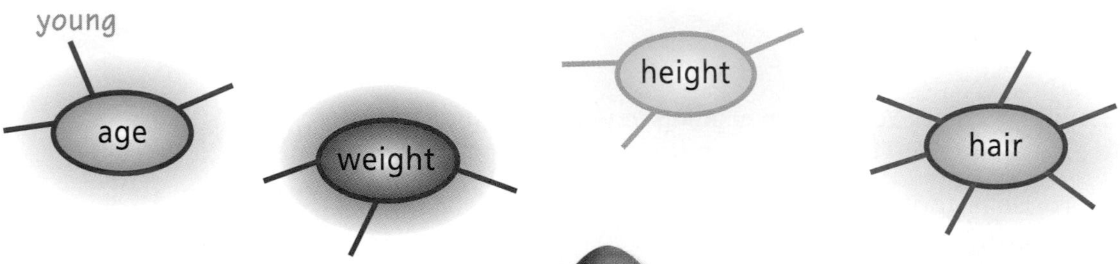

2 *PAIRS.* **Look at the photos. Take turns using the words from Exercise 1 to describe someone in the pictures. Your partner guesses which person you are describing.**

A: Tall and slim.
B: Picture A.
A: Yes!

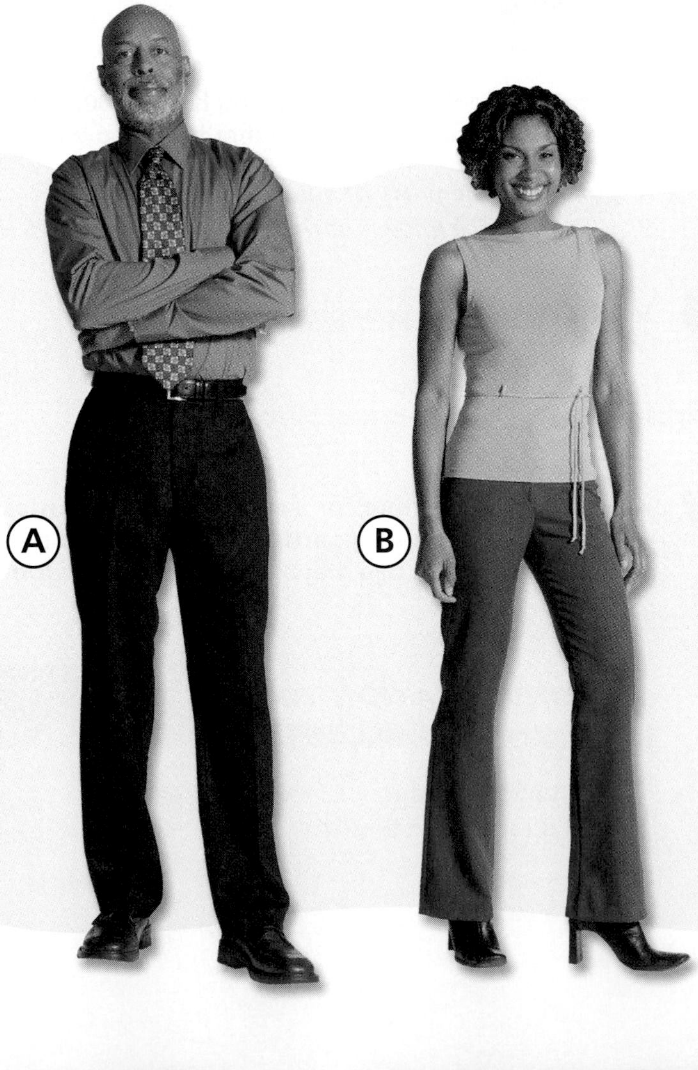

Listening

3 🎧 **Listen to the conversation between two women. They're talking about two friends, Maurice and Julia. Check (✓) the pictures of Maurice and Julia.**

Maurice

a. ☐

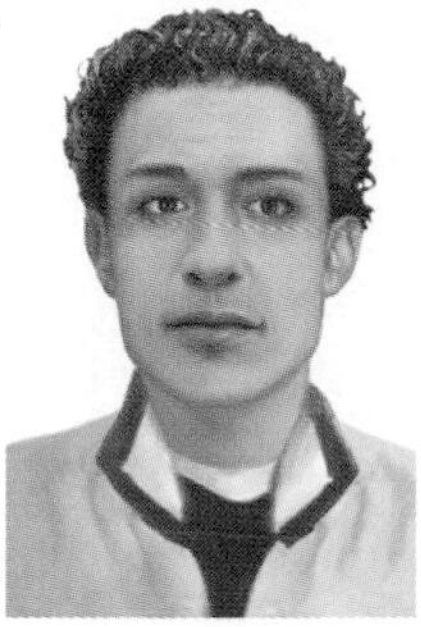

b. ☐

Julia

a. ☐

b. ☐

4 🎧 **Listen again and circle the letter of the correct answer.**

1. Maurice and Amy know each other because they ____.
   a. work in the same office
   b. are in the same English class
   c. met at a party
2. Maurice wants Cristina's phone number because he wants to ____.
   a. study English with her
   b. ask her on a date
   c. have coffee with her
3. Amy ____ give Cristina's phone number to Maurice.
   a. is going to
   b. isn't going to
   c. can't

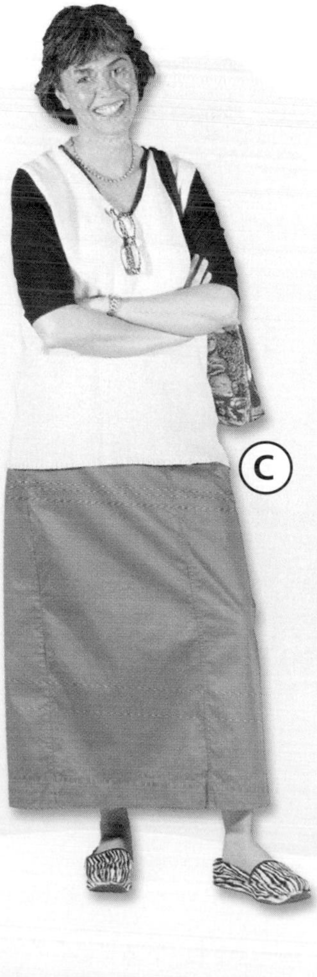

C

D

Grammar focus

1 **Study the examples of *be* and *have* for descriptions.**

He**'s** in his 20s, probably about 28.	She **has** long, straight hair.
She**'s** average height.	He **has** hazel eyes.
He**'s** quite slim.	He **doesn't have** a mustache or beard.

2 **Look at the examples again. Circle the correct verb to complete the rules in the chart.**

be/have **with descriptions**
Use ***be / have*** to talk about a person's age, height, and weight.
Use ***be / have*** to talk about a person's hair and eyes.
Note the following exception: *He* ***is*** *bald.*

Grammar Reference page 144

3 **Complete the descriptions with the correct forms of *be* or *have*. You can use contractions.**

My friend Judy and I **(1)** ___are___ both 21 years old, but she and I look completely different. I **(2)** __________ short, and she **(3)** __________ tall. I **(4)** __________ a little heavy, and she **(5)** __________ average weight. I **(6)** __________ long, curly blond hair, and she **(7)** __________ long, straight black hair.

My friends Tony and Tom are identical twins. They look exactly alike. They **(8)** __________ about 30. They **(9)** __________ black hair and brown eyes. They **(10)** __________ tall, and they **(11)** __________ slim. The only way I can tell them apart is this: Tony **(12)** __________ a mustache, and Tom **(13)** __________(not) one.

Pronunciation

4 **Listen. Notice the weak pronunciations of *and* and *or*.**

She's tall and slim.
He's average height and has black hair.
He has curly brown hair and hazel eyes.
She has long black hair and brown eyes.

I'm not tall or slim.
He isn't short or heavy.
He doesn't have a beard or mustache.
She doesn't have blond hair or blue eyes.

5 **Listen again and repeat.**

Speaking

6 *PAIRS.* **You're going to the airport to meet your partner's visitors. Take turns describing the people and finding them in the picture.**

Student A, look at page 137. Student B, look at the picture on the left. Find each person that your partner describes. Did you find the right person? Check with your partner.

A: My colleague, Sandra Vazquez, is going to arrive on Saturday. Can you meet her at the airport?

B: Sure. What does she look like?

A: She . . .

7 **Now switch roles. Student B, look at page 139.**

Writing

8 **Write a paragraph describing someone's physical appearance. Write about a family member, a friend, or a famous person. Use *be* and *have*.**

Conversation to Go

A: What does she look like?
B: She's tall and slim. She has curly brown hair and brown eyes.

UNIT 8

At the movies

Vocabulary Words related to the movies
Grammar *say* and *tell*
Speaking Talking about movies

Lesson A

Getting started

1 **Match the quotes with the photos.**

1. ___ "The best romantic movie in the history of film. A classic black-and-white movie."
2. ___ "Another fast and exciting action movie."
3. ___ "Best science fiction film ever."
4. ___ "It makes everyone laugh. A comedy for the entire family."

2 **In which photo(s) can you see . . .**

1. an actor? ________
2. an actress? ________
3. special effects? ________
4. costumes? ________

3 ***PAIRS.*** **Discuss the questions.**

What kinds of movies do you like?
Who is your favorite actor or actress?
What movies are playing now in movie theaters?
Which ones do you want to see? Why?

Reading

4 **Read the article about memorable moments in film history. Then circle the letter of the correct answer.**

1. Which movie does Tomás like?
   a. *Star Wars* b. *Casablanca*
2. Why does he like it?
   a. the actors b. the special effects
3. Which movie does Reiko like?
   a. *Star Wars* b. *Dr. No*
4. Why does she like it?
   a. the scenery b. the actor
5. Which movie does Mariana like?
   a. *Dr. No* b. *Casablanca*
6. Why does she like it?
   a. the story b. the director

"In your opinion, what are the most memorable movies in the history of film?" That's the question we asked our readers.

"I think the first *Star Wars* movie is the best science fiction film. I didn't like the new ones very much, but the original *Star Wars* is a fantastic movie. The special effects are amazing, and the story is interesting. I can't remember the names of the actors, but I love the scene where Luke fights Darth Vader." **Tomás, Mexico**

"I love James Bond movies, and my favorite is *Dr. No.* It was the first 007 movie, and although the beginning is slow, the ending is excellent. Sean Connery was the best actor who played James Bond, and he always will be." **Reiko, Japan**

"One of my favorite movies is *Casablanca*—I love old, romantic films. I think the story and the music are really good. Black-and-white films are my favorites." **Mariana, Brazil**

5 **Read the article again and check (✓) the adjective(s) used to describe things about each movie.**

	Star Wars	*Dr. No*	*Casablanca*
amazing			
excellent			
fantastic	✓		
good			
interesting			
romantic			
slow			

Grammar focus

1 Study the examples with *say* and *tell.* Underline the object.

Tomás **said** (that) he really **liked** *Star Wars*.
He **told us** (that) he **loved** the special effects.
Mariana **told me** (that) she **loved** *Casablanca*.
She **said** (that) black-and-white films **were** her favorites.

2 Look at the examples again. Circle the correct word to complete the rules in the chart.

say and *tell*
There is no object after ***say / tell***.
There is always an object after ***say / tell***.
Use the ***present / past*** after *said* and *told*.
NOTE: You can leave out the word ***that*** after ***say*** and ***tell***.

Grammar Reference page 144

3 Circle *said* or *told* in each sentence.

1. She **said / told** she liked comedies.
2. He **said / told** me he went to the movies every weekend.
3. I **said / told** that I didn't go to the movies very often.
4. Tara **said / told** Elizabeth that she loved science fiction films.
5. Elizabeth **said / told** that she hated action movies.
6. I **said / told** Carlos that I was taking a filmmaking course.
7. Carlos **said / told** me he didn't want to take the course.
8. Pete **said / told** he was late for the movies.
9. Rachel **said / told** that he had to hurry.
10. He **said / told** me his favorite actress was Halle Berry.

4 Complete the sentences. Use the correct form of *say* or *tell* and the correct form of the verb in parentheses.

1. Tomás ___told___ John that the special effects in *Star Wars* ___were___ (**be**) amazing.
2. Reiko ________ that she ________ (**love**) James Bond films.
3. She ________ me that Sean Connery ________ (**be**) a good actor.
4. She ________ that *Dr. No* ________ (**be**) her favorite Bond movie.
5. Mariana ________ her favorite film ________ (**be**) *Casablanca*.
6. She ________ us that she ________ (**like**) old films.
7. She ________ me that she ________ (**love**) the music in *Casablanca*.

Pronunciation

5 🎧 **Listen. Notice the groups of consonant sounds in the words.**

a **cl**assic **bl**ack-and-white fi**lm**
an int~~e~~**r**e**st**ing **st**ory
exc**i**ting **sp**ecial effe**cts**
He said that he li**k**~~e~~**d** *Star Wars*.
the be**st** scie**nce** fi**ct**ion movie
a **sl**ow **st**ar**t**
an e**xc**elle**nt** a**ctr**ess
She to**ld** us she lo**v**~~e~~**d** o**ld** fi**lms**.

6 🎧 **Listen again and repeat.**

Speaking

7 *BEFORE YOU SPEAK.* **Make notes about your favorite movie.**

8 *PAIRS.* **Take turns asking each other questions and telling about your favorite movie. Use your notes.**

A: *My favorite movie is a classic—* E.T. *It's a science fiction movie. I loved the story.*
B: *Who are the actors?*

9 **Tell the class what you learned about your partner's favorite movie.**

Elena's favorite movie is E.T.
She said that she loved the story.

Name of film: ______
Actor(s)/Actress(es): ______
Director: ______
Story: ______
Special effects: ______
Music: ______
Scenery: ______
Costumes: ______

Writing

10 **Write a short review of a good movie you recently saw. Include information about the actors, director, story, special effects, music, scenery, and costumes.**

CONVERSATION TO GO

A: Steve **said** he **liked** Bond movies because of the special effects.
B: Really? He **told me** he **liked** Bond movies because of the beautiful actresses!

Review 2

Units 5–8

Unit 5 Culture shock

1 Look at the list of situations. Then listen to the model conversation.

- meet a friend's parents for the first time
- pick someone up at the airport
- go to class on the first day
- go to dinner with your boss
- start a new job
- go to a job interview
- go to a friend's home for dinner
- go to a surprise birthday party

2 Choose a situation from the list in Exercise 1, but don't say it aloud. Think about the things you should and shouldn't do in that situation.

3 *GROUPS OF 4.* Play the guessing game. Take turns. Say what you should and shouldn't do in the situation you chose. Your partner will guess the situation.

Unit 6 Party time!

4 *GROUPS OF 3.* You planned a party together. Now the party is over. Look at the picture. This is the scene before the people arrived. Describe the scene.

5 Imagine that it is now last week and you are just starting to plan the party. Listen to the model conversation.

6 Role-play. Pretend that you're planning the party. You want the party to look like the picture. Take turns. Make suggestions for planning the party.

Unit 7 First impressions

7 🎧 Listen to the model conversation.

8 *PAIRS.* Student A, go to page 137. Student B, go to page 139. Look at the pictures. Take turns describing the person in each one. How many people are the same?

Unit 8 At the movies

9 🎧 Listen to the model conversation.

10 Interview five people. Find out what kind of movies they like. Take notes in the chart.

Name	Favorite kind of movie	Favorite movie	Why?

11 Report back to the class about your classmates' favorite movies.

UNIT 9

What would you like?

Vocabulary Words related to eating at a restaurant
Grammar *would like/like, would prefer/prefer*
Speaking Ordering food and drinks in a restaurant

Lesson **A**

Getting started

1 *GROUPS OF 3.* **Look at the words in the box. Find them in the photos.**

customer	fork	glass	knife	menu
napkin	pepper	salt	spoon	waiter

The Shrimp Boat

APPETIZERS

Shrimp Cocktail
Soup of the Day
Garden Salad

* * *

ENTRÉES

Shrimp Savoy
Shrimp Plaza
Shrimp Ritz

served with rice or pasta and mixed vegetables

* * *

DESSERTS

Cheesecake
Chocolate Ice Cream
Raspberry Sorbet
Coffee Tea
Cappuccino Espresso

2 **Look at the menu. Complete the sentences with the words in the box.**

~~appetizer~~	dessert	entrée
side dish	tea	

1. The soup is an appetizer.
2. The Shrimp Savoy is an __________.
3. The pasta is a __________.
4. The ice cream is a __________.
5. After your meal, you can have coffee or __________.

3 *PAIRS.* **Discuss the questions.**

How often do you go to restaurants?
What is your favorite restaurant?
Why do you like it?

Listening

4 **Look at the menu. Listen to two people ordering a meal at The Shrimp Boat. On the menu, put an *M* next to the food the man orders and a *W* next to the food the woman orders.**

5 **Listen again. Match the name of the dish with the description.**

1. Shrimp Savoy ___	a. shrimp in black olive sauce with tomatoes and herbs
2. Shrimp Plaza ___	b. shrimp in tomato sauce with herbs and olives
3. Shrimp Ritz ___	c. shrimp in herb sauce with tomatoes and olives

Grammar focus

1 Look at the examples. Write *a* or *b* in each blank.

Key:	a = what you like in general
	b = what you want now or in the future

1. **Do** you **prefer** chocolate ice cream or vanilla ice cream?
   I **prefer** chocolate. __a__
2. **Do** you **like** seafood?
   Yes, I **do**. I **like** all kinds of seafood. _____
3. **Would** you **prefer** rice or pasta?
   I'**d prefer** the rice. _____
4. What **would** you **like**?
   I'**d like** the Shrimp Savoy. _____

2 Look at the examples again. Circle *a* or *b* to complete the rules in the chart.

would like/like, would prefer/prefer	
Use __________ to talk about things you like in general.	
a. *I like* or *I prefer*	b. *I'd like* or *I'd prefer*
Use __________ to ask for something you want.	
a. *I like* or *I prefer*	b. *I'd like* or *I'd prefer*
NOTE: *I'd prefer = I would prefer; I'd like = I would like*	

Grammar Reference page 145

3 Circle the correct answers.

1. A: Would you like a table near the window?
   B: Yes, I like to sit near the window. / Yes, thank you.
2. A: Do you prefer black or green olives?
   B: I'd prefer black. / I prefer black.
3. A: Would you like to see the menu?
   B: Yes, we would, thanks. / We like the menu.
4. A: Would you prefer soup or salad?
   B: I prefer soup. / I'd prefer soup.

Pronunciation

4 **Listen to the weak and strong pronunciations of *would*. Notice the /d/ sound in *I'd like* and *I'd prefer* and the linking in *would you*.**

What would you like? — **I'd** like the shrimp.
Would you like salad? — Yes, thanks. I **would**.
Would you prefer rice or pasta? — **I'd** prefer pasta.

5 **Listen again and repeat.**

Speaking

6 *PAIRS.* **Use the cues to complete the conversation between a waiter and a customer.**

Waiter: *Order?* Would you like to order?
Customer: *The shrimp.*
Waiter: *An appetizer?*
Customer: *No.*
Waiter: *Drink?*
Customer: *Iced tea.*
Waiter: *Dessert?*
Customer: *Yes.*
Waiter: *Cake or ice cream?*
Customer: *Cake.*
Waiter: *Anything else?*
Customer: *Check, please.*

7 *GROUPS OF 3.* **Student A, you are a waiter/waitress at Rosie's Restaurant. Students B and C, you are customers. Student A, look at this page. Students B and C, look at page 142. Student A, take the customers' order. Write it on the guest check.**

Writing

8 **You're a famous chef. You're going to open a new American restaurant in your city. What would you like to have on the menu? Write a memo to the person who will design the menu. Include information about appetizers, entrées, side dishes, desserts, and drinks.**

CONVERSATION TO GO

A: **Would** you **like** the check?
B: No, thank you!

UNIT 10

Big issues

Vocabulary Global issues
Grammar *will* for predicting
Speaking Making predictions

Lesson A

Getting started

1 **Match the words on the left with the examples on the right.**

1. economy _b_
2. transportation ___
3. space ___
4. politics ___
5. population ___
6. communication ___
7. climate ___

a. United States: 288 million people
b. money, bank
c. rainy, hot
d. car, airplane, bus
e. the moon, Mars, a space station
f. phone, fax, email
g. government, president, the White House

Pronunciation

2 **Listen. Notice the stressed (strong) syllable in each word. Mark the stress.**

● climate	prediction
transportation	politics
population	communication
economy	government

3 **Listen again and repeat. Check your answers.**

4 *PAIRS.* **Look at the photos. Tell which photo matches each topic in Exercise 1.**

I think Photo A matches politics.

Reading

5 **Arthur C. Clarke is a scientist. He has also written many science fiction novels, including *2001: A Space Odyssey*. Read his predictions.**

File Edit View Favorites Tools Help

Back Forward Stop Refresh Home Search Favorites History Mail Print Edit Discuss Copernic Translate Messenger

Address http//www.bravenewworld.com.uk Go Links

Brave New World

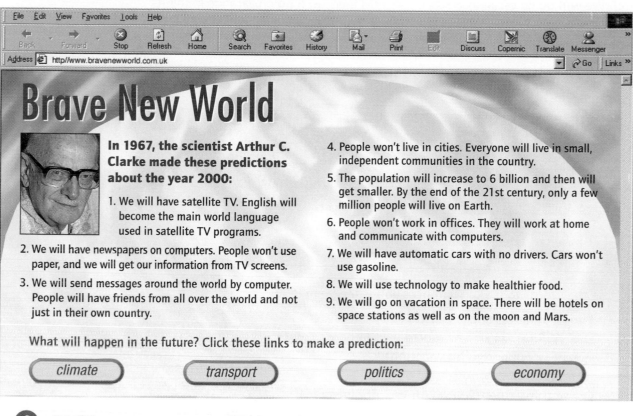

In 1967, the scientist Arthur C. Clarke made these predictions about the year 2000:

1. We will have satellite TV. English will become the main world language used in satellite TV programs.
2. We will have newspapers on computers. People won't use paper, and we will get our information from TV screens.
3. We will send messages around the world by computer. People will have friends from all over the world and not just in their own country.
4. People won't live in cities. Everyone will live in small, independent communities in the country.
5. The population will increase to 6 billion and then will get smaller. By the end of the 21st century, only a few million people will live on Earth.
6. People won't work in offices. They will work at home and communicate with computers.
7. We will have automatic cars with no drivers. Cars won't use gasoline.
8. We will use technology to make healthier food.
9. We will go on vacation in space. There will be hotels on space stations as well as on the moon and Mars.

What will happen in the future? Click these links to make a prediction:

climate *transport* *politics* *economy*

6 ***PAIRS.*** **Which of Arthur C. Clarke's predictions have come true? Put a check (✓) next to the predictions that are true for most people today.**

7 **Complete the predictions from the reading with the words in the box.**

cars	space	~~programs~~	messages	offices
cities	food	the news	population	

1. We will have satellite TV programs.
2. We will read __________ on the computer.
3. People around the world will send __________ to each other by computer.
4. No one will live in __________.
5. The __________ of the world will get smaller.
6. No one will work in __________.
7. __________ won't need drivers or gasoline.
8. The __________ we eat will be healthier.
9. There will be hotels in __________.

Grammar focus

1 **Study the examples of *will* for predicting.**

We **will go** on vacation in space.	I think we**'ll go** on vacation in space.
People **won't live** in cities.	I don't think people **will live** in cities.
What **will happen** in the future?	What do you think **will happen**?

2 **Look at the examples again. Circle the correct words to complete the rules in the chart.**

***will* for predicting**
After *will* or *won't,* use **the base form of the verb / verb + *-ing*.**
Use ***I think* + subject + won't / I don't think + subject + *will*** to predict what will not happen.

Grammar Reference page 145

3 **Use the words to make sentences about the year 2100.**

1. The population of the world / not increase.
   The population of the world won't increase.
2. Where / people / go on vacation?
3. I / not think / people / go on vacation in space.
4. Everyone / have / a computer?
5. I think / everyone / speak one language.
6. The world's weather / not get warmer.
7. You think / technology / cost less?
8. I think / transportation / be cheaper.
9. The world economy / be stronger.
10. There be / flying cars.
11. I / not think / we find life on another planet.

Speaking

4 *GROUPS OF 3.* **You are visiting a website called Y2K100. It asks you to send your predictions for the year 2100. Discuss your predictions for the topics below.**

In 2100, people will work ten hours a week.

- politics
- transportation
- clothing
- food
- work
- economy
- communication
- climate
- vacations

5 **Change groups and discuss your predictions. Are there any predictions that everyone agrees on?**

Writing

6 **Look again at the web page on page 45. Use Arthur C. Clarke's predictions as a model. Write your own web page with predictions about five big issues for the year 2050. Use *will*.**

CONVERSATION TO GO

A: In 2050, math **will** still **be** an important subject in school.

B: I hope not!

UNIT 11

Hard work

Vocabulary Activities related to work
Grammar *have to/don't have to*
Speaking Describing jobs

Lesson A

Getting started

1 **Complete the job descriptions with the words in the boxes.**

type letters and contracts	~~arrange meetings~~	make decisions

Administrative Assistant

"I work for a lawyer. My boss tells me what he needs, and I call clients to **(1)** arrange meetings. I also use a computer to **(2)** ______________. Sometimes I don't like my job because I can't **(3)** ______________. Mostly I do what my boss tells me to do."

meet with clients	travel	communicate	give presentations

Sales Manager

"I sell computer software for a large company. I have clients all over the country, and I **(1)** ______________ to different cities all the time. I like to **(2)** ______________ because I enjoy talking to people in person. When I'm traveling, I use a laptop to **(3)** ______________ about my company's products. I use my cell phone and email to **(4)** ______________ with my clients and boss when I'm on the road."

work as a team	make much money	wait on customers	work long hours

Salesperson

"I work in a large department store. I **(1)** ______________ and help them find what they are looking for. I **(2)** ______________ with other salespeople in my department. We all **(3)** ______________; for example, I work from 11:00 A.M. to 9:00 P.M., Tuesday through Sunday. We don't **(4)** ______________, but we get employee discounts on the things we buy."

2 *GROUPS OF 3.* **Talk about activities you do in your job now or want to do in a future job.**

Reading

3 **Look at the photo of the pizza delivery person. Which two activities in Exercise 1 do you think he does in his job?**

____________________ ____________________

4 **Read the article "Nine to Five." Then check your guesses in Exercise 3.**

PIZZA *To Go*

Name: Marcus Willis

Job: Pizza delivery person

Wages: $5.50/hour

Nine to Five

So you think my job is easy? You pick up the pizza, drive around town, go back to the shop, and then do it all again. It isn't that easy.

First, I don't earn much per hour, so I have to work long hours—sometimes I start at 3:00 P.M. and finish at 2:00 A.M. I also have to drive a lot. I drive about 80 miles every day, and I have to use my own car because the company doesn't give me one. That's a real problem. Another problem is the tips. Customers don't have to give me tips, but without the extra money, I don't earn much. Finally, I'm always busy. When I finish driving, I have to wait on customers in the shop and, of course, I have to be polite, even when I'm tired! Then my boss answers the phone, and I have to leave again and deliver another pizza.

The next time a delivery person brings you a pizza, remember: Does he have to work hard? Yes, he does! So be nice to him, and give him a big tip!

5 **How does Marcus feel about his job? Read the article again and write *T* (true) or *F* (false) after each statement.**

Marcus feels that . . .

1. delivering pizza is a difficult job.
2. his job pays well.
3. the pizza company should give him a car.
4. getting tips is important.
5. he isn't always busy at work.

Grammar focus

1 **Study the examples with *have to*.**

I **have to** work long hours.
He **has to** pick up the pizza.
Does he **have to** work hard? Yes, he **does**. / No, he **doesn't**.
Customers **don't have to** give him tips.

2 **Look at the examples again. Complete the rules in the chart with *is* or *isn't*.**

have to/don't have to
Use *have to/has to* + the base form of the verb when something _____ necessary.
Use *don't have to/doesn't have to* + the base form of the verb when something _____ necessary.

Grammar Reference page 145

3 **Write conversations. Use the words given and the correct form of *have to*.**

1. A: What / do / in your job? *What do you have to do in your job?*
   B: We / meet clients. *We have to meet clients.*
2. A: What / your boss / do?
   B: He / give presentations.
3. A: You / travel?
   B: Yes / do.
4. A: You / work as a team?
   B: No / not.
5. A: She / use a computer?
   B: Yes / she / answer email from customers.

Pronunciation

4 **Listen. Notice the pronunciation of *have to* ("hafta") and *has to* ("hasta").**

have to   have to work   I have to work long hours.
Does he have to work hard?

has to   has to drive   He has to drive a lot.
He has to pick up the pizza.

5 **Listen again and repeat.**

6 *PAIRS.* **Practice the conversations in Exercise 3.**

Speaking

7 *BEFORE YOU SPEAK.* **Look at the list of jobs. Add one more job to the list. Complete the chart with activities people *have to* do and *don't have to* do in these jobs. Then rank the jobs in your order of preference (1 = the best and 6 = the worst).**

Job	Has to	Doesn't have to
____ administrative assistant	type letters	meet with clients
____ doctor		
____ grocery store owner		
____ salesperson		
____ flight attendant		
____ ______________		

8 *GROUPS OF 3.* **Which jobs do you think are best and worst? Discuss your opinions and give reasons.**

A: *I think doctors have the worst job. They have to help very sick people. They have to work long hours.*
B: *I don't think they have the worst job. They don't have to . . .*

9 **Compare your group's answers with the rest of the class. Which job did most people think was the best? The worst?**

Writing

10 **Imagine that you are working in your ideal job. Write an article like the one on page 49 describing a typical day at work. Describe the activities that you *have to* do and *don't have to* do every day.**

CONVERSATION TO GO

A: **Do** you **have to make** decisions in your job?
B: Yes, I **do**. Umm . . . no, I **don't**. Well, yes . . .

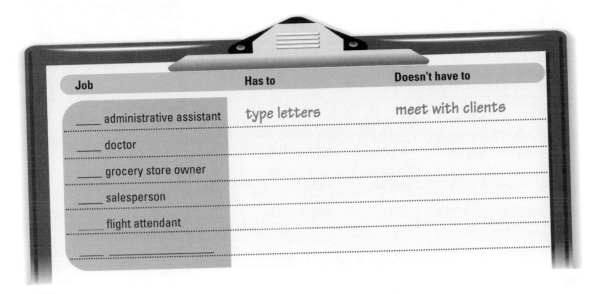

UNIT 12

Island life

Vocabulary Practical activities
Grammar Present perfect for indefinite past: *ever, never*
Speaking Talking about practical experience

Lesson A

Getting started

1 *PAIRS.* **Look at the photo of Mulkinney Island. Would you like to live there? Why?**

2 **Read the advertisement for a new television show, *Adventure Island*. Complete the sentences with the verbs in the box.**

build	catch	grow	have	make
spend	take care of	~~travel~~	work	

Adventure Island

A new reality TV show

REALITY ADVENTURE
ADVENTURE ISLAND
TELEVISION

Do you like to (1) __travel__ to new places and (2) ________ time outdoors? Are you ready to (3) ________ an adventure?

Mulkinney Island is in the north Atlantic. No one lives there. There are no houses, no stores, and no hospitals. We are looking for sixteen adventurous people from around the world to live on the island for a year.

We need people who can (4) ________ houses, (5) ________ clothes, and (6) ________ food.

We also need people who know how to (7) ________ fish, (8) ________ on a farm, and (9) ________ animals.

Send your application today. Explain why we should pick you to join us on Adventure Island!

3 *PAIRS.* **Compare your answers in Exercise 2.**

4 **What other abilities will be useful on the island? Check *Yes* or *No* and write why.**

Does *Adventure Island* need people who can . . .	Yes	No	Why?
use a computer?			
start a business?			
cook for a large group?			
write newspaper articles?			
teach a class?			

5 *PAIRS.* **Compare your answers.**

I don't think Adventure Island needs people who can use a computer. There are no computers on the island!

Reading

6 **Andrew Ho wants to be on *Adventure Island*. Read his application form. Then check (✓) *Yes* or *No* to each question about his experience.**

Name: Andrew Ho

Age: 25

1. Have you ever spent time outdoors? YES ☐ NO ☐

I've gone camping many times, and I like hiking and mountain climbing. I've also gone fishing in the ocean, and I've caught a lot of fish! I love the outdoors.

2. Have you ever worked on a farm? YES ☐ NO ☐

I haven't worked on a farm, but my family has had several pets, and I think I'm good at taking care of animals. I've had a vegetable garden, and I've grown carrots, tomatoes, and lettuce in my backyard.

3. Have you ever lived overseas? YES ☐ NO ☐

I've never lived overseas, but I've traveled abroad and around the United States. I like to travel and meet new people. I'm an adventurous person.

4. Have you ever cooked for large groups? YES ☐ NO ☐

I'm a cook in a hospital. I think this experience will be useful because I cook for large groups all the time.

7 **Discuss. Is Andrew Ho a good choice for *Adventure Island?* Why? What can he do?**

Grammar focus

1 Look again at the application form on page 53 and answer the questions.

Is Andrew growing vegetables now?
Do we know exactly when he grew vegetables?

2 Study the examples of the present perfect for the indefinite past.

I**'ve grown** vegetables in my backyard.
My family **has had** a lot of pets.
Have you **ever spent** time outdoors? Yes, I **have**. / No, I **haven't**.
I **haven't worked** on a farm.
I**'ve never lived** overseas.

3 Look at the examples again. Circle the correct words to complete the rules in the chart.

Present perfect: indefinite past; *ever, never*
Use the present perfect when the exact time of an action **is / is not** important.
Use *have* or *has* + the **present / past** participle to form the present perfect.
Use **never / ever** + present perfect to ask a question.
Use *not* or **never / ever** + present perfect to make a negative statement.
NOTE: The past participle of regular verbs is the base form of the verb + *-ed*. See page 150 for a list of irregular past participles.

Grammar Reference page 146

4 Complete the conversations with the correct present perfect form of the verbs in parentheses.

1. A: __Have__ they ever __used__ (**use**) a computer?
   B: Yes, they __have__.
2. A: ________ you ever ________ (**build**) a fire?
   B: Yes, I ________. I ________ (**go**) camping several times.
3. A: ________ she ever ________ (**take care of**) farm animals?
   B: No, she ________, but she ________ (**have**) a few pets.
4. A: ________ they ever ________ (**live**) overseas?
   B: They ________ (**not live**) overseas, but they ________ (**travel**) abroad.
5. A: ________ you ever ________ (**go**) fishing?
   B: Yes, I ________. I ________ (**go**) hiking, too.
6. A: ________ he ever ________ (**cook**) for large groups?
   B: Yes, he ________. He's a cook in a hospital.

Pronunciation

5 🎧 **Listen. Notice how a vowel sound at the end of a word links to a vowel sound at the beginning of the next word.**

Have you ever	Have you ever lived overseas?
Has he ever	Has he ever grown vegetables?
Have you ever	Have you ever spent time outdoors?
Have they ever	Have they ever used a computer?

6 🎧 **Listen and repeat.**

Speaking

7 *BEFORE YOU SPEAK.* **Look at the chart and check (✓) the activities that you have done. Then add two more activities to the chart.**

8 *GROUPS OF 3.* **Interview each other. Ask follow-up questions to get more information. Record the answers in the chart.**

A: Have you ever grown vegetables?
B: Yes, I have.
A: Really? What kind of vegetables?
B: I've grown tomatoes.

Activities	You	Classmate 1	Classmate 2
grow vegetables			
take care of animals			
go camping			
make clothes			
catch a fish			
travel overseas			

9 **Which person in your group should be on the TV show *Adventure Island*?**

Writing

10 **The TV show *Adventure Island* has invited you to apply for their next adventure. Are you ready to go? Write a letter explaining why you should go. Describe the things you have done that will help you on the island. Use the present perfect.**

Conversation to Go

A: **Have you ever made** your own clothes?
B: Yes, **I have.**

Review 3

Units 9–12

Unit 9 What would you like?

1 Listen to the model conversation.

2 *PAIRS.* Make the menu for your own American restaurant. Think of a name for the restaurant. Then think of two interesting appetizers, two entrées, two side dishes, and two desserts. Write the names of the dishes in the menu. (Be sure you can describe each dish.)

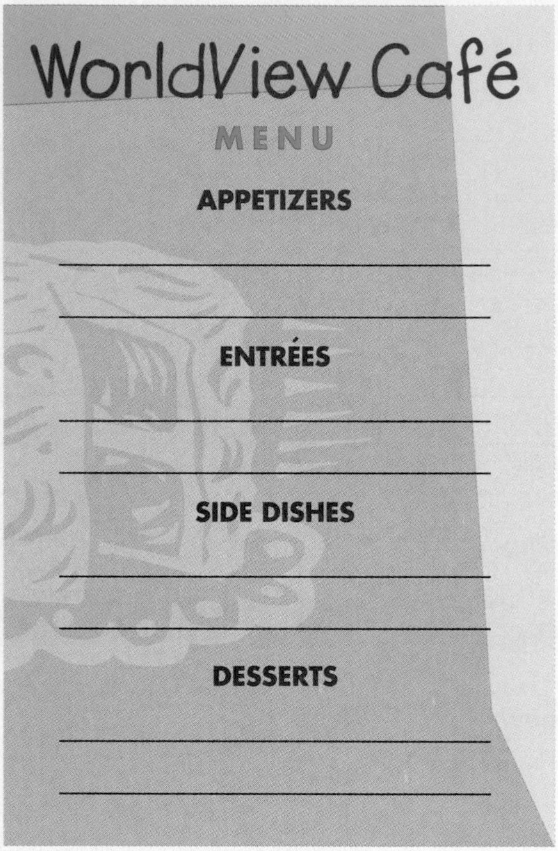

3 *PAIRS.* Find a new partner. Student A, you're the waiter; Student B, you're the customer. The waiter gives the menu to the customer and explains the dishes on it. The customer orders. Then switch roles.

4 Discuss. Which restaurant has the best or the most interesting menu?

Unit 10 Big issues

5 Listen to the model conversation.

6 Make three predictions about the future. Predict something that will happen in 20 years, in 50 years, and in 100 years. Write your predictions on the timeline.

7 Walk around the room. Tell one of your predictions to a classmate, and ask if he or she agrees with it. If your classmate agrees, you get one point. Continue telling classmates your predictions. The person with the most points at the end of the game is the winner.

8 Share your results with the class. Which predictions did the most people agree with? Which did they disagree with?

Unit 11 Hard work

9 Listen to the model conversation.

10 *GROUPS OF 3.* Student A, think of a job. Students B and C, ask *Yes/No* questions about the job. When you have enough information, guess what job it is. Keep track of the number of questions you ask. Take turns until everyone thinks of a job and everyone asks and answers questions. The person whose job requires the most questions wins.

Unit 12 Island life

11 Listen to the model conversation.

12 Check (✓) at least six activities that you have done. (You can use your imagination.)

☐  Name: ________	☐  Name: ________	☐  Name: ________	☐ 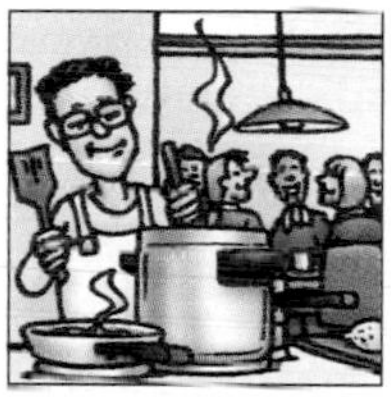 Name: ________
☐  Name: ________	☐  Name: ________	☐  Name: ________	☐  Name: ________
☐  Name: ________	☐  Name: ________	☐  Name: ________	☐  Name: ________

13 Take turns asking *Yes/No* questions to find out what experience your classmates have. When you find someone who answers yes, write the student's name in the appropriate box. The person with the most names filled in at the end of the game is the winner.

World of Music 2

Wonderful Tonight

Eric Clapton

Vocabulary

1 *PAIRS.* **Match each verb with the correct word or phrase.**

1. ask _c_	a. "yes"
2. brush ___	b. her a present
3. feel ___	c. him a question
4. give ___	d. me sit down
5. go ___	e. the lights
6. help ___	f. to a party
7. put on ___	g. with me
8. say ___	h. wonderful
9. turn off ___	i. your hair
10. walk around ___	j. your makeup

The 70s

The "British invasion" of rock 'n' roll was in full swing in the 70s. ***Eric Clapton****, a guitar virtuoso, became—and remains—one of rock music's most admired stars.*

Listening

2 **Listen to the song. Put the pictures in order.**

1. _____ 2. _____ 3. _____

A

B

C

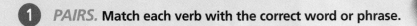

3 Listen to the song again. Complete the lyrics.

Wonderful Tonight

It's late in the evening.
She's wondering what clothes to wear.
She ___________ her makeup
and ___________ her long blonde hair.
And then she ___________ me, "Do I look all right?"
and I ___________, "Yes, you look wonderful tonight."

We ___________ to a party
and everyone ___________ to see
this beautiful lady,
who's ___________ around with me.
And then she ___________ me, "Do you feel all right?"
and I say, "Yes, I ___________ wonderful tonight."

I feel wonderful because I see the love light in your eyes,
and the wonder of it all, is that you just don't realize how much I love you.

It's time to ___________ home now
and I've got an aching head.
So I ___________ her the car keys
and she ___________ me to bed.

And then I ___________ her,
as I ___________ the light,
I say, "My darling, you were wonderful tonight."
"Oh, My darling, you were wonderful tonight."

4 *PAIRS.* **Compare your answers in Exercise 3.**

Speaking

5 *GROUPS OF 3.* **Discuss the questions.**

What is the song about? Tell the story.

What do you like about the song (for example, the words, the music, the singer's voice)?

Is there something you don't like?

UNIT 13

Keepsakes

Vocabulary Possessions; phrasal verbs related to possessions
Grammar Review: possessive *'s*; possessive adjectives/pronouns; *belong to*
Speaking Talking about special possessions

Lesson A

Getting started

1 **Look at the photos of the keepsakes. What do you think *keepsakes* are?**

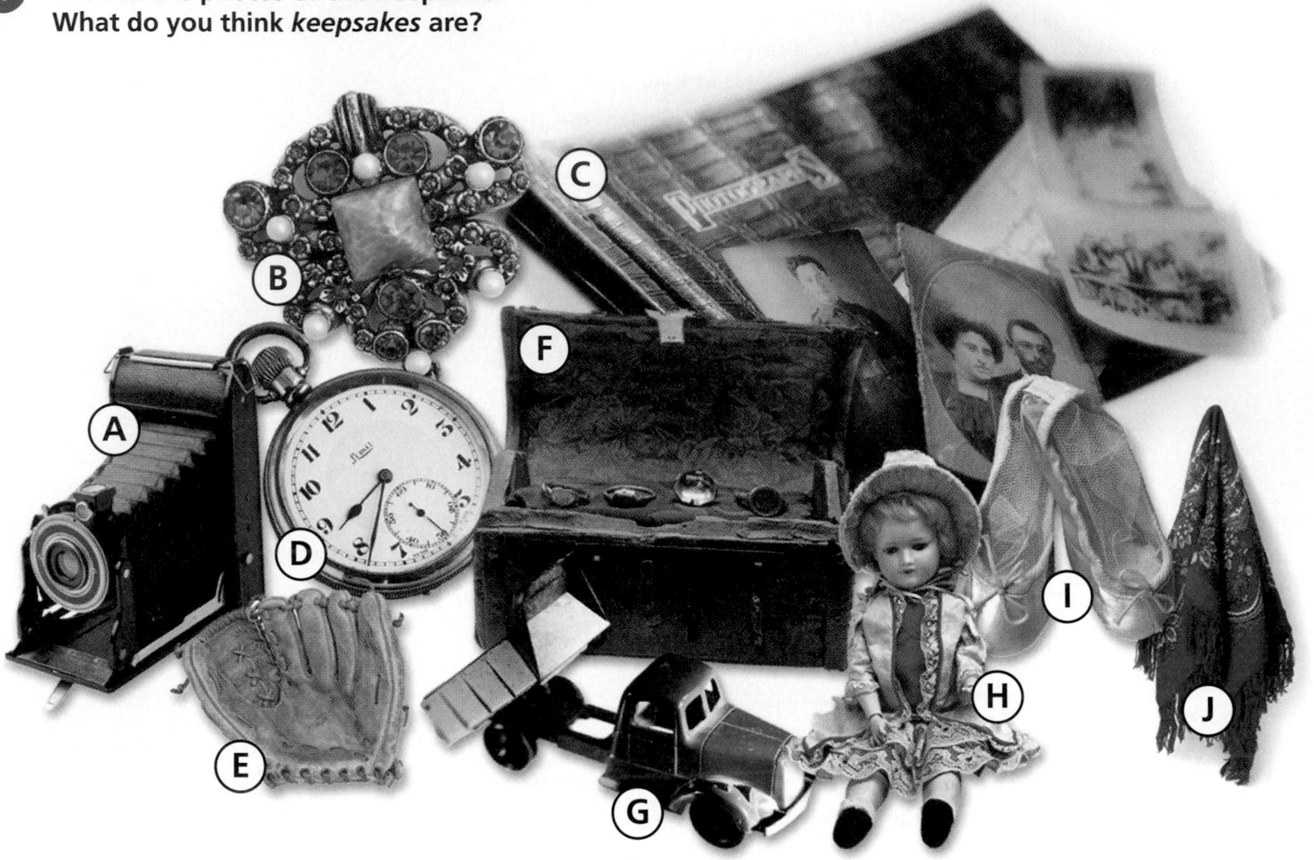

2 **Match the words in the box with the photos.**

1. ballet shoes I	2. baseball glove ___	3. camera ___	4. doll ___
5. jewelry box ___	6. photo album ___	7. pin ___	8. shawl ___
9. toy truck ___	10. watch ___		

3 **Listen and check your answers. Then listen and repeat.**

4 *PAIRS.* **Discuss. What things do you keep as keepsakes?**

Listening

5 **Match the phrasal verbs with their meanings.**

1. give away g
2. put away ____
3. try on ____
4. pass on ____
5. take out ____
6. fall apart ____
7. throw away ____
8. fall out ____

a. separate into small pieces
b. wear a piece of clothing for a short time to see if it fits
c. put something in the garbage
d. drop out of the place where it belongs
e. put something in the place where it is usually kept
f. remove something from a place
g. give something to someone instead of selling it
h. give something to someone else

6 **Mr. Freeman and his young daughter, Lisa, are talking. Listen to their conversation. Circle the letter of the correct answer.**

1. What are Mr. Freeman and Lisa doing?
   a. taking things out of a trunk b. putting things away in a trunk
2. Are the things old or new?
   a. old b. new

7 **Listen again. Match each keepsake in the trunk with the person it belongs (or belonged) to.**

1. jewelry box
2. watch
3. photo album
4. baseball glove

a. Lisa's mother
b. Lisa's father
c. Lisa's grandmother
d. Lisa's grandfather

Pronunciation

8 **Listen. Notice the stress and linking in these phrasal verbs.**

Take it **out**.

Don't give it a**way**.

It's falling a**part**.

I'll try it **on**.

Let's throw it a**way**.

Wait! Something is falling **out**.

9 **Listen again and repeat.**

10 *PAIRS.* **Discuss the questions.**

When you don't need something anymore (clothing, books, furniture), what do you do? Do you put it away and keep it, throw it away, or give it away to someone? Why?

Grammar focus

1 **Study the examples. Notice the ways to express possession. Notice the use of the apostrophe (').**

Possessive *'s*	Possessive adjective	Possessive pronoun	*belong to* + object pronoun
	It's **my** baseball glove.	It's **mine**.	It **belongs to me**.
These are **Grandma's** dolls.	They're **her** dolls.	They're **hers**.	They **belong to her**.
This is **George's** watch.	It's **his** watch.	It's **his**.	It **belongs to him**.
That's the **neighbors'** car.	It's **their** car.	It's **theirs**.	It **belongs to them**.

2 **Look at the examples again. Circle the correct words to complete the rules in the chart.**

Possessive *'s*; possessive adjectives/pronouns; *belong to*
To show possession:
Use a possessive adjective (*my, your, his, her, our, their*) **before / after** a noun.
Use a possessive pronoun (*mine, yours, his, hers, ours, theirs*) **alone / before a noun**.
Add *'s* to a **singular / plural** noun.
Add *'* to a **singular / plural** noun that ends in *s*.
Use **an object pronoun / a possessive pronoun** after *belong to*.

Grammar Reference page 146

3 **Circle the correct words to complete the sentences.**

1. That's not her doll. It's **our / ours.**
2. This isn't **me / my** sweater. Is it **your / yours**?
3. These are my **parent's / parents'** books.
4. This photo album belongs to **her / she**.
5. My sisters don't like to clean **their / her** room.
6. Is this **her / hers** book? Or is it **him / his**?
7. These old clothes **belong / belongs** to **they / them**.

4 **Rewrite the sentences using the words in parentheses.**

1. This doll belonged to your grandmother. (your grandmother)
   This was your grandmother's doll.
2. That's my photo album. (belong to)
3. This is your mother's dress. (hers)
4. Their car is very old. (my grandparents)
5. Where is Jason's house? (his)
6. These are our CDs. (belong to)
7. I like to look at her pictures. (Lucia)

Speaking

5 *BEFORE YOU SPEAK.* **Imagine you are filling a trunk with keepsakes of the people in your class. Your teacher will give you the name of a classmate. Choose one thing that reminds you of that person, such as a piece of clothing that the person wears a lot or something that the person always has.**

6 *GROUPS OF 4.* **Talk about the keepsakes that you chose. As a group, agree on one thing to put in the trunk to remember each person by.**

A: I think we should put Julia's blue sweater in the trunk. She wears it a lot.
B: No, I think we should put in her cell phone. She loves to talk on the phone after class.

Person	Keepsake
Julia	Cell phone

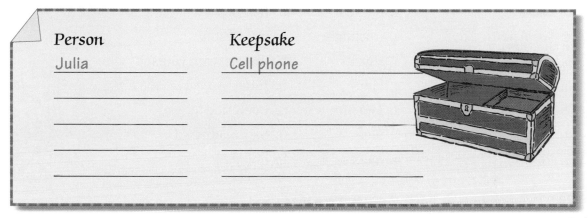

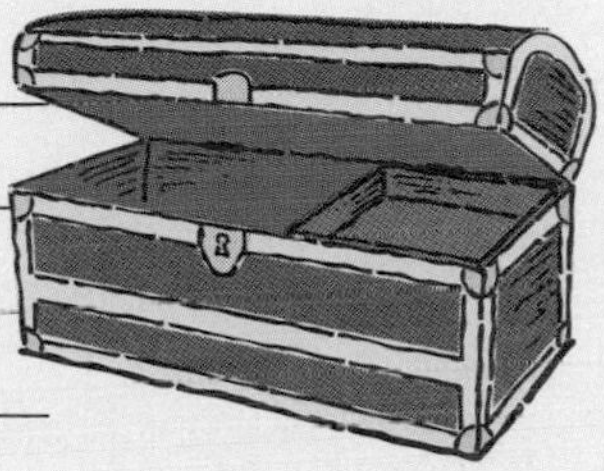

7 **Each group writes the list of keepsakes (with no names!) on the board or reads it to the class. Others in the class guess the people who go with each keepsake. Give reasons.**

Anna: *The first thing on our list is a cell phone.*
José: *I think it's yours. You like talking on the phone.*
Anna: *No, it's not mine.*
María: *I think it's Julia's. She uses her phone more than anyone!*
Anna: *You're right. The cell phone belongs to Julia.*

Writing

8 **Think of a keepsake that belongs to you or to a member of your family. Write a paragraph describing the keepsake and the person, thing, or event it reminds you of. Use possessive forms.**

Conversation to Go

A: Is this **your** phone?
B: No, it's **Susan's**. **Mine** is at home.

UNIT 14

Tales of Nasreddin Hodja

Vocabulary Adjectives describing feelings and behavior
Grammar Adverbs of manner; comparative adverbs
Speaking Describing actions

Lesson A

Getting started

1 **Choose the correct synonym for each adjective.**

1. upset _a_	a. unhappy	b. happy
2. embarrassed ____	a. comfortable	b. ashamed
3. calm ____	a. relaxed	b. nervous
4. suspicious ____	a. trusting	b. not trusting
5. proud ____	a. shy	b. pleased with yourself
6. polite ____	a. kind	b. rude
7. absent-minded ____	a. forgetful	b. interested
8. rude ____	a. nice	b. bad-mannered
9. loud ____	a. quiet	b. noisy

A

2 **Listen and check your answers. Then listen and repeat.**

3 *PAIRS.* **Nasreddin Hodja is a character from Turkish folktales. Look at the pictures. Use adjectives from Exercise 1 to describe how Hodja and the other men look.**

In Picture A, Hodja looks calm, and the men look suspicious.

B

D

C

Reading

4 **Think about folktales you know. What's their purpose?**

5 **Read the stories. Then match the paragraphs with the pictures.**

Hodja, the King

One day, Nasreddin Hodja was walking down the road. He was looking at the sky absent-mindedly and not watching where he was going. Suddenly, he bumped into a man. B

"Do you know who I am?" the man shouted angrily. "I am the King's advisor!"

"That's very nice," said Hodja calmly. "As for me, I am a king." ____

"A king?" asked the man suspiciously. "What country do you rule?"

"I rule over myself," said Hodja proudly. "I am king of my emotions. I never get angry as you did just now."

The man apologized and walked away quickly, feeling very embarrassed.

Eat, My Coat, Eat

A friend invited Nasreddin Hodja to a banquet. He went to the banquet wearing his everyday clothes. ____

Everyone, including his friend, was very rude to him, so Hodja left quickly. He went back home, put on his best coat, and returned to the banquet. Now everyone greeted him more politely than before and invited him to sit down and eat.

When the soup was served, Hodja put the sleeve of his coat in the bowl. He said loudly, "Eat, my coat, eat!" ____

His friend angrily asked Hodja to stop.

"When I came here in my other clothes," said Hodja calmly, "you treated me badly. But when I returned wearing this fine coat, you gave me the best of everything. So I thought that you wanted my coat, not me, to eat at your banquet!"

6 **What lessons do these stories teach? Choose the best answer for each story.**

1. "Hodja, the King"
   a. Some people are more important than others.
   b. It is important to control your anger.
   c. Everyone gets angry at times.

2. "Eat, My Coat, Eat"
   a. True friends are not rude to each other.
   b. Wear clothes that are right for the occasion.
   c. Look at the person, not at his or her clothes.

Grammar focus

1 **Study the examples of adverbs of manner.**

Hodja walked **absent-mindedly** down the road.
The man walked away **quickly**.
Everyone greeted him **more politely than** before.
The man shouted **angrily**.

2 **Look at the examples again. Circle the correct words to complete the chart.**

Adverbs of manner
Use adverbs of manner to describe **how / why** something is done. Use *more* + adverb + *than* to compare two **actions / things**. Many adverbs are formed by adding *-ly* to **a verb / an adjective**. For adjectives ending in *-y,* change the *y* to **a / i** before adding *-ly*.
NOTE: Some adverbs such as *fast*, *hard*, and *early,* have the same form as adjectives.

Grammar Reference page 146

3 **Complete the sentences with adverbs of manner. Form the adverbs from the adjectives in parentheses.**

1. Nathan walked __happily__ down the street. (happy)
2. The man sat __________ in front of the house. (quiet)
3. "Where did you go?" the little girl asked the little boy __________. (suspicious)
4. "I designed that building," the architect said __________. (proud)
5. The man shouted __________ at his neighbor. (angry)

4 **Complete the sentences. Use the comparative form of the adverbs in the box. Include *than* when necessary.**

calmly	comfortably	~~loudly~~	politely	quickly

1. John is quiet. Janet is loud. Janet speaks __more loudly than__ John.
2. Eduardo never rushes. Roberto is always in a hurry. Roberto does everything ________________ Eduardo.
3. The salesperson wasn't rude, but the customer was. The salesperson behaved ________________ the customer.
4. Sam was angry when he heard the news. Jennifer wasn't upset about the news. Jennifer reacted ________________ Sam.
5. Just after his operation my friend was in a lot of pain, but now he's resting ________________.

Pronunciation

5. Listen. Notice the stressed (strong) syllable in each word.

angrily　　suspiciously　　quietly　　comfortably

6. Listen again. This time, notice the pronunciation of the vowels shown in blue. They all have the short, unclear sound /ə/. Then listen again and repeat.

7. Now listen to these words. Draw a circle over the stressed syllables and underline the vowels that have the short, unclear sound /ə/.

happily　　politely　　nervously　　hungrily

8. Listen again and repeat. Check your answers.

Speaking

9. *GROUPS OF 4.* Work together to tell a folktale that teaches something. Decide which folktale you'd like to tell, and take notes. Take turns telling different parts. Add or change parts of the folktale to make it as funny or dramatic as you like.

Folktale:
Characters:
Setting:
Main events:
Ending:
Lesson:

10. Share your folktale with the class. What does each folktale teach?

Writing

11. Write a short story or folktale you know. Use adverbs of manner.

CONVERSATION TO GO

A: You speak **quickly**!
B: No, I don't. You just listen **more slowly** than I speak!

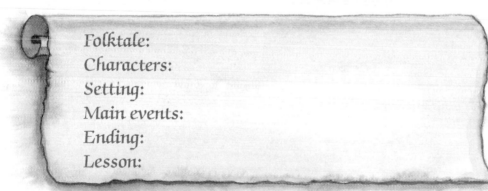

UNIT 15

Popular sports

Vocabulary Sports
Grammar Verbs for likes/dislikes + noun/verb + *-ing*
Speaking Talking about sports you like doing

Lesson **A**

Getting started

1 **Match the words with the pictures.**

1. aerobics A
2. basketball ____
3. biking ____
4. jogging ____
5. karate ____
6. swimming ____

2 **Write the sports in the box next to the correct verbs in the word webs.**

aerobics	basketball	~~biking~~	golf	hockey	jogging
karate	skiing	soccer	swimming	tennis	volleyball

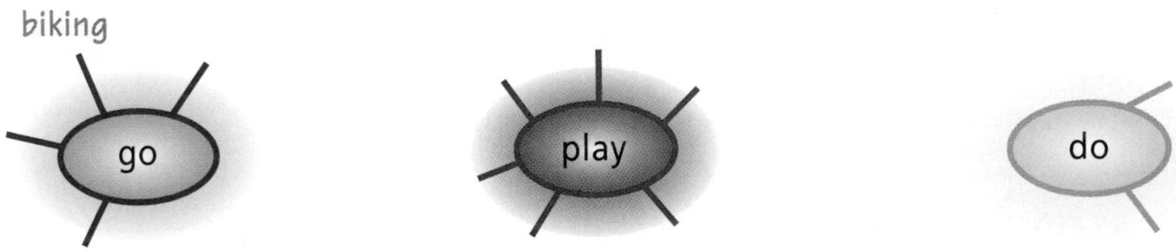

3 🎧 **Listen and check your answers. Then listen and repeat.**

4 ***PAIRS.*** **Discuss the questions.**

Which sports do you like to play?
Which sports do you like to watch?

Listening

5 **Listen to the TV report about sports in Canada. How popular are the sports in the box? Write each sport in the correct place in the graph.**

baseball	basketball	~~golf~~	hockey	swimming	volleyball

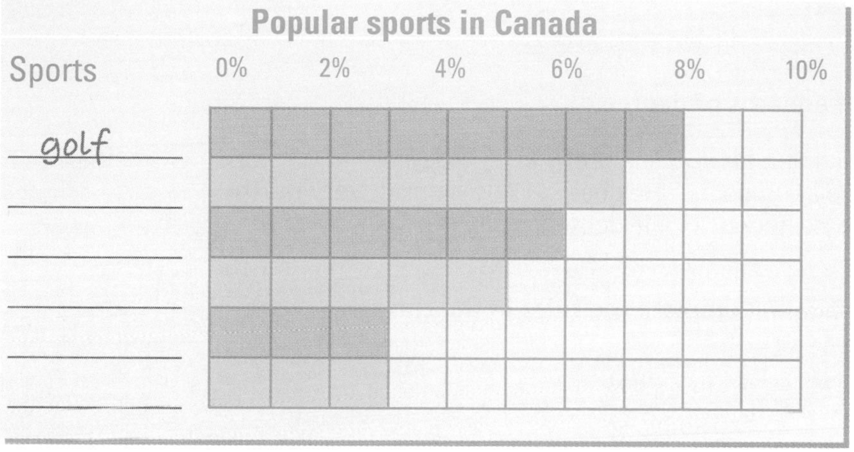

6 **Listen to the rest of the interview and check (✓) who like playing each sport.**

	Mostly women	Mostly men	Equal men and women
golf	☐	✓	☐
hockey	☐	☐	☐
volleyball	☐	☐	☐
swimming	☐	☐	☐
baseball	☐	☐	☐
basketball	☐	☐	☐

7 *PAIRS.* **Discuss these questions. In your country who likes team sports more, men or women? Who likes individual sports more?**

Grammar focus

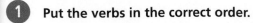

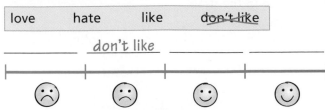

1 **Put the verbs in the correct order.**

love	hate	like	~~don't like~~

_______ don't like _______ _______

2 **Study the examples of adverbs of degree.**

Some men like playing golf **a lot**.
Some men **really** like playing golf.
Some women **really** hate hockey.
She **really** loves volleyball.
He doesn't like swimming **very much**.
He doesn't **really** like swimming.

3 **Look at the examples again. Complete the rules in the chart.**

Adverbs of degree
Use *a lot* with _______ to add emphasis.
Use _______ with *like, love,* and *hate* to add emphasis.
Use _______ and _______ with *not like* to reduce the negative meaning of a sentence.

Grammar Reference page 147

4 **Complete the conversations with the correct form of the words in parentheses.**

1. A: What sports do you like doing **(like/do)**?
   B: I don't really like sports **(really not like/sports)**, but I love swimming **(love/swim)**.
2. A: Do your parents do any exercise?
   B: My father _______ **(love/play basketball)**, and my mother _______ **(like a lot/play golf)**.
3. A: Do you like jogging?
   B: No, I _______ **(hate/jog)**. I think it's boring.
4. A: Do your brothers _______ **(like/play)** any sports?
   B: Well, they _______ **(not like very much/play soccer)**. They're not very good at it!
5. A: Do you _______ **(like/do aerobics)**?
   B: Yes, I do. I go to a class before work.
6. A: Does your boyfriend _______ **(like/ski)**?
   B: Yes, he _______ **(really love/it)**. He goes every weekend.

Pronunciation

5 🎧 **Listen. Notice the way stress is used to contrast or compare ideas.**

Do you like **ski**ing? — Yes, I **love** skiing.
Do you like playing **golf**? — No, I **hate** playing golf.
Women liked **swim**ming, and men liked **bas**ketball.
My **sis**ter likes doing ae**ro**bics, and my **broth**er likes playing **soc**cer.

6 🎧 **Listen again and repeat.**

7 *PAIRS.* **Practice the conversations in Exercise 4.**

Speaking

8 *BEFORE YOU SPEAK.* **Write five more sports on the chart.**

9 **Take a survey.**

Ask six students in the class how they like each sport. Give one point for each person who likes the sport, and two points for each person who loves the sport.

A: Do you like swimming?
B: Yes, I love it. (2 points)

	Student/Points					
Sport	A	B	C	D	E	F
swimming		2				

10 **Discuss the questions.**

What is the most popular sport in your class?
Do men and women like different sports?

Writing

11 **Write a paragraph. Choose a sport that you love or hate. Explain how you feel about the sport and why. Use verbs for likes/dislikes and adverbs of degree.**

Conversation to Go

A: Do you **like jogging**?
B: No, I **hate jogging**, but I **love watching** TV!

UNIT 16

Food for thought

Vocabulary Food
Grammar Quantifiers + count/non-count nouns
Speaking Talking about what you eat

Lesson A

Getting started

1 **Match the words with the photos.**

1. bread B
2. chocolate ____
3. cookies ____
4. fruit ____
5. juice ____
6. lettuce ____
7. onions ____
8. oranges ____
9. salt ____
10. strawberries ____
11. vegetables ____
12. water ____
13. yogurt ____

2 **Listen and check your answers. Then listen and repeat.**

3 *PAIRS.* **Discuss. Which foods in Exercise 1 do you like? Which do you dislike? Why?**

Pronunciation

4 **Listen to the words. Notice the pronunciation of the vowel. Write each word in the correct sound group.**

Soup /u/	Sugar /ʊ/

5 **Listen and check your answers. Then listen again and repeat.**

6 *PAIRS.* **Take turns asking these questions.**

Which foods are good for you?
Is fruit good for you?
Are cookies good for you?
Is juice good for you?

WVUE Radio

6.00 P.M. FOOD FOR THOUGHT!
Listen to the latest information on health and nutrition, and find out what we should and shouldn't eat!

Listening

7 Look at the chart. Are the foods in the first column good for you or bad for you? In the second column, write *good* or *bad*. In the third column, write your reasons.

	Your opinion	Why?	Host's opinion	Why?
chocolate	bad	makes you fat	good	live longer
salt				
bread				
potatoes				
fruit				
coffee				
tea				

8 *PAIRS.* Compare your answers.

9 Listen to the radio show *Food for Thought!* Does the host think the foods listed in Exercise 7 are good for you or bad for you? In the fourth column of the chart, write *good* or *bad*.

10 Listen again. In the last column, write the reasons for the host's opinions.

Grammar focus

1 **Study the examples of the quantifiers with count and non-count nouns.**

much/many, a little/a few, a lot of	
(+) I eat	**a little** bread. **a few** potatoes. **a lot of** fruit/vegetables.
(–) I don't eat	**much** bread. **many** cookies.
(?) How **much** bread How **many** potatoes	do you eat?

some/any

(+) I have **some** bread/potatoes every day.
(–) They don't have **any** tea/cookies in their house.
(?) Do you have **any** chocolate/cookies?

2 **Look at the examples again. Fill in the blanks with *some, any, a little, a few, a lot of, much,* and *many*.**

Quantifiers + count/non-count nouns
Use ________ in questions and negative statements. Use ________ to talk about a large quantity. Use ________, ________, and ________ with count nouns (e.g., potatoes, oranges). Use ________, ________, and ________ with non-count nouns (e.g., bread, salt).

Grammar Reference page 147

3 **Underline the correct words in the conversations.**

1. A: How **much / many** strawberries did you eat last week?
   B: I ate **much / a lot of** strawberries. I didn't leave **some / any** for you!
2. A: Do you buy **any / many** fruit?
   B: Yes. I like to have **a lot of / many** fruit in the house.
3. A: How **much / many** tomatoes do you usually put in a salad?
   B: Not **much / many**. I use just **a little / a few**.
4. A: How **much / many** bread do you buy each week?
   B: I don't eat **a little / much** bread. I'm on a diet.
5. A: Do you drink **much / many** tea?
   B: No, and I don't drink **some / any** coffee either.
6. A: Do you eat **much / many** potatoes?
   B: Yes, I eat **much / a lot of** potatoes.

4 *PAIRS.* **Take turns asking and answering the questions in Exercise 3. Give true answers.**

Speaking

5 *BEFORE YOU SPEAK.* **Look at the foods in the first column in the chart. How much of each do you eat for each meal? Write *some, a little, a lot of, not many,* or *not much* for each one.**

	Breakfast	Lunch	Dinner	Snack
Meat				
Poultry (chicken, turkey)				
Fish and seafood				
Bread, pasta, and rice				
Dairy (milk, cheese)				
Beans				
Vegetables				
Fruit				
Sweets (cake, candy)				

6 *GROUPS OF 3.* **Take turns talking about what you usually eat. Discuss what's good and bad about the foods you eat.**

I have bread for breakfast and lunch. I guess I eat a lot of bread every day! I don't think it's bad for me. Sometimes I put a little butter or a little cheese on it. I don't eat much meat, and I don't eat many cooked vegetables. But I eat a lot of fruit and salad. That's healthy, isn't it?

7 **How similar or different are everyone's diets? Who has the healthiest diet?**

Writing

8 **Write a paragraph. What is your advice for healthy eating? Which foods should people eat a lot of? Which foods should people try not to eat? Which foods are good and bad to eat? Why? Use the quantifiers *some, any, much, many, a little, a few, a lot of.***

CONVERSATION TO GO

A: Do you eat **much** fruit?
B: Yes, I eat **a lot of** fruit, but I don't eat **many** vegetables.

Review 4

Units 13–16

Unit 13 Keepsakes

1 Listen to the model conversation.

2 Think of a keepsake that you or your family has. Where is it from? What does it look like? Why is it important to you?

3 *PAIRS.* Student A, talk for two minutes. Tell Student B about your keepsake. Explain as many details as you can. Student B, don't ask questions, just listen. Then switch. Student B, talk for two minutes about your keepsake.

4 Change partners. This time you each have only one minute. Talk about the keepsake.

5 Change partners again. This time you each have only thirty seconds. Talk about the keepsake.

Unit 14 Tales of Nasreddin Hodja

6 Listen to the model conversation.

7 Write each adverb below on a small piece of paper. Fold all the pieces of paper in half, put them in a box, and mix them up.

happily	quickly	calmly	proudly
sadly	angrily	nervously	shyly
slowly	thoughtfully	respectfully	rudely
politely	absent-mindedly	suspiciously	hungrily

8 *GROUPS OF 4.* Make up a group story. Take turns picking a piece of paper. Add two sentences to the story using the adverb on your paper. Continue until all the papers are gone. The person who uses the last adverb finishes the story.

9 Share your stories with the class. Which group has the most unique story?

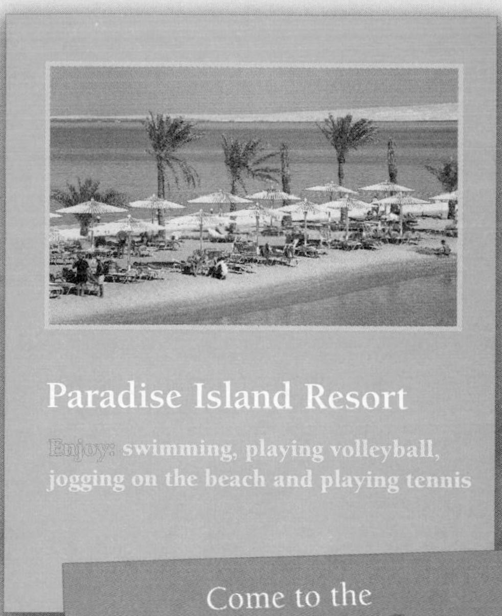
Paradise Island Resort
Enjoy: swimming, playing volleyball, jogging on the beach and playing tennis

Come to the
BLUE MOUNTAIN CLUB
SUMMER SPORTS
biking
hiking

Sports Plus Club
Relax and get in shape with:
• doing aerobics • playing basketball
• golf or soccer • doing karate

Unit 15 Popular sports

10 🎧 Listen to the model conversation. Look at the ads.

11 *GROUPS OF 3.* Your group has just won a free weekend to a resort.

Student A, you really love the outdoors, and you like doing sports outside in any weather. You like hiking and skiing, but you hate aerobics. You don't like playing volleyball or golf.

Student B, you really like the sun, and you hate doing exercise inside. You love jogging, but you don't like hiking. You don't like doing aerobics or karate.

Student C, you really love doing aerobics. You don't like doing sports in very hot or very cold weather. You like doing karate a lot. You hate volleyball and hiking.

Look at the ads. Discuss which sports you love, like, don't like, or hate doing. Then as a group, decide which resort to go to.

Unit 16 Food for thought

12 🎧 Listen to the model conversation.

13 *PAIRS.* Imagine that you and your partner are roommates.

Student A, you're at the supermarket. Call Student B to ask what you should buy. Write a shopping list on a piece of paper.

Student B, look at page 142. Tell Student A what food you have at home and what Student A needs to buy at the supermarket.

14 Switch roles. Student B, call Student A to ask what you should buy. Write a shopping list. Student A, look at page 140.

UNIT 17

A nice place to work

Vocabulary Office practices
Grammar Modals: *have to/had to* for present and past necessity
Speaking Talking about obligations

Lesson **A**

Getting started

1 **Look at the photo. Where do you think the people are?**

2 *PAIRS.* **Look again at the photo. Describe the clothes the people are wearing.**

3 **Complete the sentences with the words in the box.**

break	casual
commute	downsize
flextime	formal
~~full-time~~	part-time
supervisor	telecommute

1. I have a ___full-time___ job. I work forty hours a week.
2. When I get tired, I take a __________ from work and get some coffee.
3. I wear jeans to work. My office has a __________ dress code.
4. My __________ manages about twenty employees.
5. Janet has a __________ schedule. She works different hours every day.
6. My neighbors __________ to work by train—two hours each way.
7. Marco's office is somewhat __________, so he wears a suit and tie to work.
8. Raymond works only 20 hours a week, but he's happy having only a __________ job.
9. I work from home; in other words, I __________. I stay in touch with the office by email, telephone, and fax.
10. My company is going to __________, so many of us are going to lose our jobs.

4 *PAIRS.* **Compare your answers in Exercise 3. What kind of dress code does the office in the photo have?**

Listening

5 *PAIRS.* **Discuss the questions.**

How do people dress in offices in your country?

Do people call their co-workers by their first names or by their titles and last names (for example, *Ms. Marino*)?

How often do people take breaks? When?

6 **Listen to an interview with a businessman. Check (✓) the topics that the interviewer asks him about.**

❑ clothing
❑ amount of work
❑ work relationships
❑ work schedule
❑ vacation time

7 **Listen again and write *T* (true) or *F* (false) after each statement.**

1. Tom Banks works in New York. T
2. He works in a bank.
3. He wears a suit to work every day.
4. He likes casual Fridays.
5. He calls his supervisors by their first names.
6. He can work at different times of the day.
7. He doesn't always work in the office.
8. The office practices at his company are the same as twenty years ago.

Grammar focus

1 **Study the examples with *have to* and *had to*.**

Present	Past
(+) Today, I **have to work** longer hours.	Twenty years ago, I **had to wear** a suit every day.
(–) We **don't have to wear** suits and ties.	We **didn't have to work** long hours.
(?) **Does** he **have to go** to the office every day? Yes, he **does.** / No, he **doesn't**.	**Did** you **have to spend** money on expensive suits? Yes, I **did.** / No, I **didn't**.

2 **Look at the examples again. Complete the rules in the chart.**

Modals: *have to/had to* for present and past necessity
Use ___________ when something is required in the present.
Use ___________ when something was required in the past.

Grammar Reference page 147

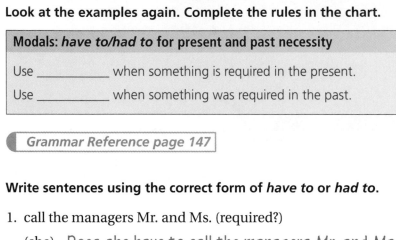

3 **Write sentences using the correct form of *have to* or *had to*.**

1. call the managers Mr. and Ms. (required?)
   (she) Does she have to call the managers Mr. and Ms.?
2. work from 9 A.M. to 5 P.M. (not required)
   You ____.
3. wear business clothes before 1996 (required?)
   (they) ____?
4. carry a cell phone at all times (required)
   He ____.
5. wear business clothes (not required)
   She ____.
6. speak many languages (required?)
   (you) ____?
7. go to the office every day last year (not required)
   We ____.
8. arrive early yesterday morning (required)
   They ____.
9. have a computer at home (required?)
   (I) ____?

Pronunciation

4 **Listen. Notice the short, weak pronunciation of the word *to* when it comes before another word and the stronger pronunciation when it comes at the end of a sentence.**

I had to wear a suit to the office.
But now I don't have **to**.
I don't have to wear a suit to work.
I can work from 11 to 7 if I want **to**.

I had to work from 9 to 5.
I don't have to go to the office every day.
But I have to work longer hours!

5 **Listen again and repeat.**

Speaking

6 *BEFORE YOU SPEAK.* **Think about work or school. Write two things you have to do and two things you don't have to do. Look at the list for ideas. Put an asterisk (*) next to the things that are different from 50 years ago.**

- the clothes you/others wear
- what you call your clients/co-workers/teachers
- the times you work or study
- the place(s) you work or study
- the way you work or study

Things you have to do:

___

Things you don't have to do:

___

7 *PAIRS.* **Ask questions about the things on your list.**

A: (clothes) *What do people wear to work at your company?*
B: *Now most people wear casual clothes. They don't have to wear suits.*

Writing

8 **Write to an American friend who is coming to work in an office in your country. Tell him or her about work practice. Write about clothes, schedules, breaks, and work relationships. Use *have to/had to* to describe necessity.**

CONVERSATION TO GO

A: **Do** you **have to wear** a suit to work?
B: No, I **don't**. But in my last job, I **had to wear** one every day.

UNIT 18

Hollywood mystery

Vocabulary Words related to police investigations
Grammar Simple past and past continuous
Speaking Describing activities in the past

Lesson A

Getting started

1 **Match the words to the pictures.**

intruder	police officer	suspect	thief	victim	witness

A

B

C

2 *PAIRS.* **Compare your answers.**

3 **Match each verb with its meaning.**

1. get arrested _e_
2. confess ____
3. investigate ____
4. question ____
5. report ____

a. tell the police about a crime
b. try to find out the truth about a crime
c. ask someone questions about a crime
d. admit that you have done something wrong
e. be taken away by the police because they believe the person is guilty of a crime

4 **Read the newspaper article. Answer the questions.**

1. Who are the victims?
2. Who is investigating the crime?
3. Were there witnesses to the crime? Did anyone question the witnesses?
4. Who is the thief?
5. Did someone get arrested for the crime?

Stolen Necklace!

HOLLYWOOD An intruder stole a valuable diamond necklace from the house of movie director Richard Price. The necklace belonged to Mr. Price's wife. Police think that the Prices' security system wasn't working when the thief entered the house. Several people saw a man running away from the house after the theft. Police want to question this man.

5 *PAIRS.* **Compare your answers.**

Reading

6 **The police questioned the people at the Prices' house the night of the robbery. Read the people's statements. Where was each person? What were they doing when the necklace was stolen?**

Richard Price (husband)

I was watching TV in the living room when I heard a loud noise from my study. I saw that the safe door was open and the necklace wasn't there! I ran outside and saw a man. He was running away from the house. He was wearing a blue jacket.

Camille Price (wife)

I was reading a book in the bedroom when I heard the sound. Then I looked out the window, and someone was running away. He was wearing a baseball cap. Then I went down to the study and saw Richard, and he told me my necklace was gone!

Brad Price (son)

I was in my room upstairs with my sister Jill. We were playing video games. I heard a loud noise and looked out the window. It was dark, but we saw a man outside. He was wearing white sneakers, and he was running away from the house. My sister stayed upstairs. When I went downstairs, my dad was calling the police and my mom was looking in the safe.

Martha McGuire (cook/housekeeper)

I was cleaning up after dinner when I heard a sound. I thought it was a car. When I looked out the kitchen window, a man was running into the trees. He was holding something in his hand. The necklace, I guess. I'm just glad the kids were upstairs!

When the necklace was stolen...	Richard Price	Camille Price	Brad Price	Martha McGuire
Where was . . . ?				
What was he or she doing?				

7 **Look at the pictures and read again the four witnesses' descriptions of the man running away. Circle the picture of the man that the witnesses described.**

Ⓐ

Ⓑ

Ⓒ

Grammar focus

1 **Look at the examples. Underline the past continuous verbs.**

We **were playing** video games upstairs when we **heard** a loud noise.
I **saw** a man outside. He **was running** away from the house.
When I **went** downstairs, my dad **was calling** the police.

2 **Look at the examples again. Circle the correct words to complete the explanations in the chart.**

Simple past and past continuous
The action in the simple past started **before / after** the action in the past continuous.
The action that started first **was / wasn't** finished before the second action started.

Grammar Reference page 147

3 **Complete the stories with the correct form of the verb in parentheses. Use the simple past or the past continuous.**

1. I was taking out (**take out**) the trash when I ________________ (**hear**) a dog barking. There ________________ (**be**) a man in someone's backyard. When I ________________ (**see**) him, he ________________ (**run**) into the trees. He ________________ (**wear**) a dark jacket and a baseball cap.

2. I ________________ (**get**) something from my car in the driveway. My neighbor and I ________________ (**talk**). We ________________ (**not/look**) at the Prices' house, so we ________________ (**not/see**) anything.

3. I ________________ (**drive**) home when I _________ (**pass**) the Prices' house. A few police officers ________________ (**stand**) in front of the house, and two officers _________ (**talk**) to Richard. The police cars ________________ (**block**) the street, so I ________________ (**drive**) home another way.

Pronunciation

4 **Listen. Notice the weak pronunciation of *was* and *were*.**

We were playing video games.

My parents were standing in the study.

They were waiting for the police.

Our housekeeper was working in the kitchen.

A man was running away.

He was wearing sneakers.

5 **Listen again and repeat.**

Speaking

6 *BEFORE YOU SPEAK.* **Are you a good witness? Someone robbed a jewelry store. Look at the picture for a few minutes. Notice what everyone in the picture is doing and what each is wearing.**

7 *PAIRS.* **Turn to page 140. Try to answer the questions together. Don't look back at the picture! When you finish the questions, look at the picture again and check your answers.**

Writing

8 **Think of a memorable event in your life. Write a paragraph about the event, describing what you and others were doing at the time.**

Conversation to go

A: What **were** the police **doing** at your house yesterday?
B: They **were asking** questions about a robbery.

UNIT 19

Bargain hunters

Vocabulary Stores and purchases
Grammar *because, for,* and infinitives of purpose
Speaking Giving reasons

Lesson A

A 1
REDBOOK
REDBOOK

B ___

C ___

Getting started

1 **Match the place names with the photos.**

1. a convenience store _C_
2. a newsstand ___
3. a drugstore ___
4. a coffee house ___
5. a restaurant ___
6. a hair salon ___
7. a clothing store ___

BARGAIN HUNTERS
Three shoppers . . . One shopping list
Who can find the best bargains?
A TV game show that COUNTS!
BARGAIN HUNTERS
Weekdays at 2:00 P.M. on Channel 6

2 *PAIRS.* **Which of the places in Exercise 1 do you go to most often?**

A: I go to a coffee house most often. I go there every day!
B: Not me. I go to a newsstand every day.

3 **Where can you get these things? Write the place next to each item. (You can get some things at more than one place.)**

1. a cup of coffee _a convenience store_
2. a haircut
3. a candy bar
4. a bottle of aspirin
5. perfume
6. sandwiches
7. socks
8. a blouse
9. a magazine
10. a shampoo and blow-dry

4 *PAIRS.* **Compare your answers in Exercise 3.**

Pronunciation

5 **Listen. Notice the stress in these compound nouns. When two words come together to make a compound noun, which part has the main stress?**

newsstand   coffeehouse   hair salon

6 **Listen again and repeat.**

7 *PAIRS.* **Mark the main stress in these compound nouns.**

drugstore   clothing store   haircut
candy bar   convenience store

8 **Listen and check your answers. Then listen and repeat.**

Listening

9 *GROUPS OF 3.* **Look at the advertisement for the new TV game show *Bargain Hunters* on page 86. Discuss these questions. What is a bargain hunter? Would you like to be a contestant on this TV show? Why?**

10 **Courtney was a contestant on *Bargain Hunters*. Listen to Courtney describe her shopping trip. Number the places in the photos in Excercise 1 in the order she visited them.**

11 **Listen again. Look at Courtney's shopping list. Write the amount she spent next to each item.**

BARGAIN HUNTERS

SHOPPING LIST

Contestant: Courtney

magazine	$3.95
aspirin	______
haircut	______
coffee	______
blouse	______
candy bar	______
Chinese food	______

Grammar focus

1 **Study the examples. Notice the ways to express reasons.**

Action	**Reason**
I went to the coffeehouse	**because** I wanted a cup of coffee. **for** a cup of coffee. **to get** a cup of coffee. **to relax**.

2 **Look at the examples again. Complete the rules in the chart with *because*, *for*, or the infinitive of purpose (*to* + verb).**

Giving reasons: *because*, *for*, infinitives of purpose
________________ is always followed by a noun.
________________ is usually followed by a clause.
________________ is sometimes followed by a noun.

Grammar Reference page 147

3 **Use the information in parentheses to rewrite the sentences.**

1. She went on vacation because she wanted a rest. (for)
   She went on vacation for a rest.
2. He joined the club because he wanted to make new friends. (infinitive)
3. They bought some chicken because they wanted it for dinner. (for)
4. I stopped at the gas station to buy some gas. (because)
5. I bought some stamps to put in my stamp collection. (for)
6. She came into the living room to get a chair. (because)
7. They went to the gym because they wanted to play basketball. (infinitive)

4 **Complete the sentences with *to*, *for*, or *because*.**

1. She went to a restaurant ___to___ have lunch.
2. He bought his grandmother a gift __________ it was her birthday.
3. We are going to the park __________ a walk.
4. She went to the store __________ buy some milk.
5. I bought this dress __________ it was on sale.
6. We went to the post office __________ get some stamps.
7. She called the doctor's office __________ an appointment.

Speaking

5 *BEFORE YOU SPEAK.* **Where do you go in a typical week? Write a list of five places. Write the reasons you go to each place.**

Place	Reasons to go there
1. convenience store	because I'm hungry; to get something sweet; for a newspaper
2.	
3.	
4.	
5.	

6 *PAIRS.* **You're going to play a guessing game. Take turns. Choose one place on your list. Say one reason you go there. Your partner will guess the place. If your partner doesn't guess correctly, give one more reason. Play three times. The person with the lowest total score wins. (one guess = one point)**

A: I go there because I'm hungry.
B: A restaurant?
A: No. I go there to get something sweet.
B: A bakery?
A: No. I go there for a newspaper.
B: A convenience store!
A: That's right! You have three points.

Scorecard

YOU	YOUR PARTNER
1. ___	1. ___
2. ___	2. ___
3. ___	3. ___
TOTAL ___	TOTAL ___

7 **Who in the class has the lowest total score?**

Writing

8 **Write an article about five of your favorite stores or restaurants. Give reasons why you go there. Use *because*, *for*, and infinitives of purpose.**

CONVERSATION TO GO

A: Why did you go to the hair salon?
B: **For** a haircut—and **to see** the hairstylist!

UNIT 20

A long run

Vocabulary Words related to the theater
Grammar *a/an, the*
Speaking Talking about the theater

Lesson A

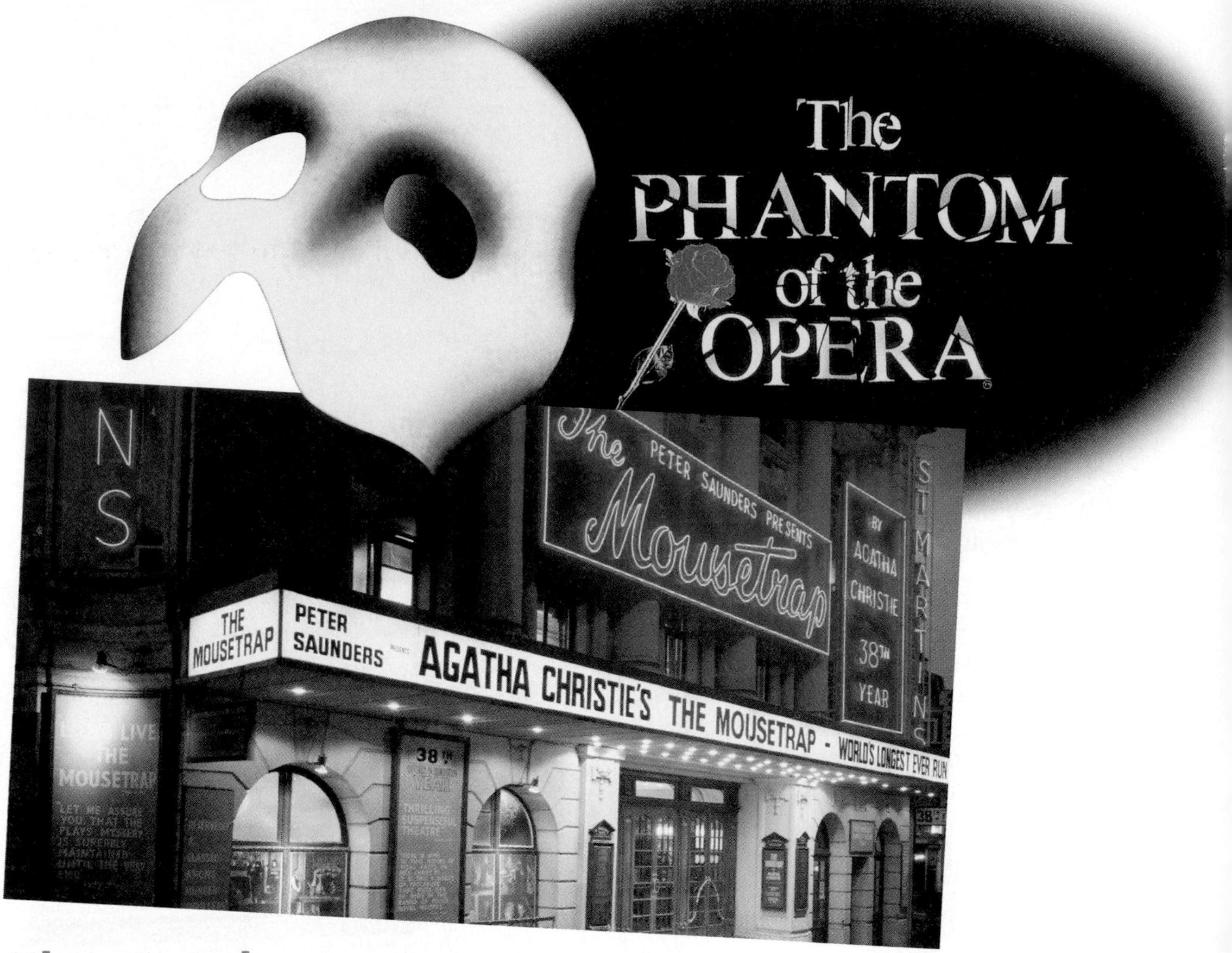

Getting started

1 **Underline the correct words to complete the sentences.**

1. The Globe is the name of a **theater / playwright** in London.
2. Actors perform in **plays / games**.
3. In **an opera / a musical**, the performers sing all the words.
4. The **spectators applaud / audience applauds** at the end of the play.
5. The **playwright / composer** writes the music.
6. The most expensive **seats / chairs** are at the front of the theater.

2 *PAIRS.* **Discuss the questions.**

Do you prefer seeing a play or a movie? Why?
Can you name any famous English-language musicals or plays?
Do you know any famous playwrights?

Reading

3 *PAIRS.* **Look at the pictures on page 90. Which do you think is a musical? Which do you think is a mystery?**

4 **Read the web article "Long Theater Runs" and complete the chart.**

	The Phantom of the Opera	*The Mousetrap*
date of first performance	1986	1952
type of show		
how it ends		
reasons for popularity		

@ Theater Online

TheaterOnline.com

MUSICALS PLAYS COMEDIES OPERA BALLET

LONG THEATER RUNS

The Phantom of the Opera

Andrew Lloyd Weber is the most successful writer of musicals in England, and "Phantom" is his most successful musical. Since it opened in London in 1986, it has played in 18 countries and more than 58 million people have seen it.

The Phantom is a young composer with an ugly face. He hides his face behind a mask and lives in the Paris Opera House. He falls in love with a beautiful opera singer named Christine, but the opera singer loves Raoul. The Phantom makes her choose: "Come with me and Raoul lives. Choose Raoul and he dies." She goes with the Phantom, but in the end he helps Christine and Raoul to be together.

Audiences love the costumes, the scenery, the story, and the music.

The Mousetrap

Agatha Christie's most famous murder mystery is the world's longest-running play. *The Mousetrap* opened in London in 1952, and there have been more than twenty-thousand performances since then.

In the play, a man and his wife have an old house. They turn the house into a small hotel. After some guests arrive, it snows and nobody can leave. A police officer arrives and says one of the people in the house is a murderer. During the play, the audience tries to figure out who the murderer is.

So what makes this more popular than other murder mysteries? Well, the play has a very surprising ending, and the murderer asks the audience to keep it a secret. Amazingly, they do. So if you want to know who did it, you have to go and see the play!

Grammar focus

1 Study the examples with *a*, *an*, and *the*.

The Mousetrap is **the** longest-running play.
A couple has **an** old house.
They turn **the** house into **a** hotel.
You have to see **the** play.
The ending is very surprising.

2 Look at the examples again. Complete the rules in the chart with *a*, *an*, or *the*.

a/an, the		
Use	_________	the first time you talk about something.
Use	_________	to talk about the same thing again.
Use	_________	when there is only one.
Use	_________	with superlative adjectives.

Grammar Reference page 148

3 Complete the article with *a*, *an*, or *the*.

Romeo and Juliet
(A Summary)

Romeo and Juliet is **(1)** ___the___ most popular of Shakespeare's plays. **(2)** _________ story is about **(3)** _________ young woman and **(4)** _________ young man who fall in love. **(5)** _________ young man is named Romeo, and **(6)** _________ young woman is named Juliet.

Their families are enemies, so they get married in secret. Romeo gets into **(7)** _________ fight and kills **(8)** _________ young man. **(9)** _________ young man is Juliet's cousin. Romeo has to leave **(10)** _________ city. Juliet sends him **(11)** _________ message. **(12)** _________ message is very important because it explains how they can stay together. But Romeo never gets **(13)** _________ message. Because of this, Romeo and Juliet both kill themselves at **(14)** _________ end of **(15)** _________ play.

Pronunciation

4 🎧 **Listen to the examples in Exercise 1. Notice the pronunciations of *a*, *an*, and *the*.**

5 🎧 **Listen again and repeat.**

Speaking

6 *BEFORE YOU SPEAK.* **Think of an interesting play or movie that you have seen. Think about the answers to these questions.**

Was it a play or a movie?
Who were the actors in it?
What was it about?
Why did you like it?

7 *GROUPS OF 3.* **Take turns. Describe the play or movie to your group, but don't say its name. Your partners will try to guess the name.**

A: It's about a teenage Indian girl.

B: Monsoon Wedding!

A: No. She meets a young British woman. The woman plays . . . .

Writing

8 **Write the story of the musical *West Side Story*. Use the cues.**

- modern-day *Romeo and Juliet*, set in New York
- young man (Tony) / fall in love / young woman (Maria)
- Tony / in a street gang (the Jets)
- Maria's brother / in another street gang (the Sharks)
- Jets / Sharks / enemies
- Jets / Sharks / fight
- a Jet / kill / Maria's brother
- then a Shark / kill / Tony

CONVERSATION TO GO

A: I saw **a** play last night.
B: How was it?
A: **The** story was interesting, but **the** acting was awful.

Review 5

Units 17–20

Unit 17 A nice place to work

CAREERS

Building Manager
- supervise ten employees
- order repairs
- meet with new tenants

Bookstore Salesperson
- wait on customers
- look up titles in the computer
- work weekends

Chef
- create new menus
- cook food
- supervise wait staff

Teacher
- teach English to children ages 6-12
- have a college degree
- start work at 7:00 A.M.

Designer
- design clothing for women
- travel to fashion shows
- have experience in the fashion industry

Computer Technician
- go to clients' offices
- install computer systems
- fix broken computers

1 Listen to the model conversation and look at the job ads.

2 *PAIRS.* Look at the job advertisements. Decide on a job to talk about.

3 *PAIRS.* Role-play a job interview. Student A, you're the job applicant. Student B, you're the interviewer. Student A, explain what you had to do in your last job. Student B, explain what Student A has to do in this job.

4 Switch roles and choose another job from the ads. Do another role-play.

Unit 18 Hollywood mystery

5 Listen to the model conversation.

6 *GROUPS OF 4.* Students A and B, you are police officers trying to solve a robbery. You have five minutes to prepare to talk to the suspects. Make a list of questions to ask the suspects about what they were doing on the night of the robbery.

Students C and D, you are suspects in the robbery. You say that you were together when it happened, so you can show that you are innocent. You have five minutes to prepare for the police officers' questions. Decide exactly what you were doing on the night of the robbery.

7 Student A, interview Student C. Student B, interview Student D. Conduct the interviews on opposite sides of the room so the suspects can't hear each other's answers! Students A and B, take notes.

8 Compare interviews. Students A and B, talk about your notes. Do you believe Students C and D were together during the robbery? Students C and D, talk about the police officers' questions. Did you give the same answers?

Unit 19 Bargain hunters

9 Listen to the model conversation and look at the picture.

10 *GROUPS OF 4.* Student A, say one place in the picture. Give a reason for going there. Student B, repeat Student A's information. Then say a new place and give a new reason. Students C and D continue. Go around the group two times. You can't repeat a place.

Unit 20 A long run

11 Listen to the model conversation and look at the pictures.

12 *GROUPS OF 3.* Make up a group story about the pictures. Take turns adding two sentences to the story. Give names to the characters and describe what is happening in the pictures. You can talk about the pictures in any order.

World of Music 3

Matter of Time

Los Lobos

The 80s

Many American musicians began exploring music of other cultures in the 80s, and some celebrated their own roots. ***Los Lobos*** *(Spanish for The Wolves) are a Los Angeles-born group with their own distinct Tex-Mex style.*

Vocabulary

1 Complete the sentences with the words in the box.

be	believe	feel like
make	~~send~~	worry

1. I'm not going to take you with me now. I'll __send__ for you when I get there.
2. You don't need anyone's help. __________ in yourself.
3. Don't __________ about me. I'll be fine.
4. This is a great party. I don't __________ going home.
5. I wish you could come with me, but we'll __________ together soon.
6. Be quiet. Don't __________ a sound.

Listening

2 Listen to the song. Circle *a* or *b* to complete the sentences.

1. The song is a conversation between ____.
   a. two friends
   b. a husband and wife
2. The singer is going to ____ home soon.
   a. leave
   b. come
3. He thinks the future will be ____ than the present.
   a. better
   b. worse

3 Listen again. Circle the correct words or phrases to complete the song.

Matter of Time

Speak softly.
(**I won't** / **Don't**) wake the baby.
Come and hold me once more,
Before I (**have to** / **can**) leave.
Hear (**there isn't** / **there's**) a lot of
work out there.
Everything (**is** / **will be**) fine.
And (**I sent** / **I'll send**) for you, baby.
Just a matter of time.

Our life,
The only thing we (**know** / **knew**).
Come and tell me once more,
Before you (**need to** / **have to**) go.
But (**there's** / **there'll be**) a better
world out there,
Though it don't feel right.
(**Will** / **Does**) it feel like our home?
Just a matter of time.
And (**I'm hoping** / **I hope**) this song
we sing's,
Not another empty dream.
(**There was** / **There's**) a time for you
and me,
In a place living happily.

[repeat]

Walk quietly.
(**I didn't** / **Don't**) make a sound.
Believe in what (**you've done** /
you're doing),
I know we (**won't** / **can't**) be wrong.
Don't worry about a thing,
(**We'll be** / **We're**) all right.
And (**we're** / **we'll be**) there with you,
Just a matter of time.

And (**we'll** / **we can**) all be together,
Just a matter of time.
Matter of time
Matter of time

(**We can** / **We'll**) be together,
In a matter of time.
You and me,
In a matter of time.
Feel like a home,
Matter of time.

4 *PAIRS.* **Compare your answers in Exercise 3.**

Speaking

5 *GROUPS OF 3.* **Discuss the questions.**

1. Why do you think the man has to leave? Where is he going?
2. What is the feeling of the song: sad, happy, hopeful, angry? Explain.
3. What does the expression "just a matter of time" mean in the song?

   a. We have to be patient and wait for a while.
   b. We don't have to wait because things will happen quickly.

UNIT 21

Long life

Vocabulary Time expressions
Grammar Present perfect: *how long/for/since*
Speaking Talking about how long you have done something

Lesson A

Getting started

1 *PAIRS.* **Look at the photos in the article. How old are the women in the pictures? Guess.**

2 **Match the expressions on the left with the similar expressions on the right.**

1. over ten years __e__	a. two days ago
2. the day before yesterday _____	b. two months
3. ages _____	c. December 31
4. a couple of months _____	d. 12:00 P.M.
5. noon _____	e. more than ten years
6. New Year's Eve _____	f. a long time

Pronunciation

3 **Listen. Notice the pronunciation of the voiceless *th* sound /θ/ in the words in the first row and the voiced *th* sound /ð/ in the words in the second row.**

thirty-first	three	month
there	more than	the day

4 **Listen again and repeat.**

5 **Listen to the question and answers. Then listen and repeat.**

When did you start work there?
- In 2002.
- When I was twenty-three.
- The beginning of the month.
- More than three months ago.
- On Thursday, the 30th.

Reading

6 **Read the article. Then match the women's names with their jobs.**

1. Dodo Cheney _____
2. Carmen Dell'Orefice _____
3. Omara Portuondo _____

a. singer
b. tennis player
c. model

Life after 70

Today, not all people over 70 think they're old. People stay younger for longer. Three women who are over 70 and still going strong, are Omara Portuondo, Dodo Cheney, and Carmen Dell'Orefice. What do they do, and how long have they done it?

Cuban singer **Omara Portuondo** is one of the most popular jazz singers in the world. She has sung in clubs and cabarets for over 50 years and was on a Buena Vista Social Club album. Now she is 73 years old and is still one of the star singers at the famous Tropicana Club in Havana, Cuba.

Dodo (Dorothy) Cheney is an 86-year-old tennis champion. She has played tennis for more than 70 years. Now she plays in tournaments for people over 75 and she has won over 320 matches.

Carmen Dell'Orefice is 71 years old. She has been a model since she was 13. Her career started 58 years ago when a photographer saw her on a bus and asked to take her photo. Today she still works for the Ford modeling agency.

7 **Read the article again. Complete the information about the three women.**

1. Omara Portuondo is _________ years old.
2. She has been a singer for more than _________ years.
3. The kind of music Omara sings is _________.
4. Dodo Cheney is _________ years old.
5. She has been a tennis player for more than _________ years.
6. She has won more than _________ tennis matches.
7. Carmen Dell'Orefice is _________ years old.
8. She has been a model for more than ________ years.
9. She began working as a model after a _________ saw her on a bus.

8 ***PAIRS.*** **Discuss the questions.**

What's your reaction to the stories about the three women in the article?

When you are their age, will you have a job?

Grammar focus

1 **Look at the examples of the present perfect with *how long*, *for*, and *since*. Answer the questions.**

How long **has** Dodo Cheney **played** tennis?
She**'s played** tennis **for** 70 years.
How long **has** Carmen Dell'Orefice **been** a model?
She**'s been** a model **since** she was 13.

1. When did Dodo Cheney start playing tennis? ____________ ago.
2. Does she play tennis now? ____________
3. When did Carmen Dell'Orefice start working as a model? ____________
4. Is she a model now? ____________

2 **Look at the examples again. Circle the correct words to complete the rules in the chart.**

Present perfect: *how long/for/since*
Use the present perfect for actions that started in the **present / past** and continue in the **present / past**. Use **for / since** with a period of time (for example, *an hour*, *two months*, *50 years*). Use **for / since** with a point in time (for example, *2:00 P.M.*, *June 25, 1953*).
NOTE: Use contractions with the subject pronouns and the verb *have*. For example, ***I've** been an engineer since 2002. **He's** worked in that office for two years.*

Grammar Reference page 148

3 **Read the information. Use the present perfect with *for* or *since* to write new sentences.**

1. He became a dancer when he was twelve. He is a dancer now.
   He's been a dancer since he was twelve.
2. He started teaching piano 38 years ago. He teaches piano now.
3. I started playing jazz in 1958. I play jazz now.
4. I have a guitar. I bought it in 2002.
5. They got married 50 years ago. They are married now.
6. She started playing tennis 70 years ago. She plays tennis now.
7. She started a new job on January 10. She works there now.
8. We started to study English last year. We study English now.
9. They live in Australia. They moved there eight years ago.

Speaking

4 *BEFORE YOU SPEAK.* **Ask yourself the questions. Write your answers in the *You* column.**

YOU	YOUR PARTNER
Where / live? I live in . . .	
How long? I've lived there . . .	
Where / work?	
How long?	
What / interested in?	
How long?	
What / study?	
How long?	
What / favorite possession?	
How long?	

5 *PAIRS.* **Now ask your partner the same questions. Write the information about your partner in the chart.**

A: *Where do you live?*
B: *In Mexico City.*
A: *How long have you lived there?*
B: *Since 1998.*

6 **Tell the class one interesting fact about your partner.**

Writing

7 **Think about a person you know well. Answer the questions in Exercise 4 about this person. Then use your answers to write about the person. Use the present perfect with *for* and *since*.**

CONVERSATION TO GO

A: How long **have you been** married?
B: **For** two months!

UNIT 22

Job share

Vocabulary Words related to tasks in an office
Grammar Modals for requests and offers
Speaking Making and responding to requests and offers

Lesson A

Getting started

1 **Complete the sentences with the verbs in the box.**

arrange	do	file	get	have	leave	make (2x)	~~send~~	sign

1. I need to <u>send</u> a fax to Paula. Do you have her fax number?
2. Did you _________ the email from Sam?
3. Can I _________ a message for Ms. Parker, please?
4. Can you _________ the meeting notes, please? The folders are over there.
5. I'll be there in a minute. I have to _________ a call first.
6. Sorry, but I can't _________ the copying now. I'm too busy.
7. Can you _________ your name here, please? Right next to the *X*.
8. What time should we _________ the meeting?
9. Let's _________ a meeting for next Friday.
10. I need to _________ a reservation at La Scala for tomorrow at 7:30 P.M.

2 *PAIRS.* **Discuss. Which of the tasks in Exercise 1 have you done?**

Reading

3 **Look at the ad. What do you think *job share* means?**

4 **Read the ad. Answer the question.**

What are the three ways you can share a job?

JOB SHARE

Do you love your job but want to work only part-time? Then maybe a job share is right for you. With a job share, you and your job-share partner can share one full-time job. This can work different ways.

- You work in the morning, and your partner works in the afternoon.
- You work Monday to Wednesday morning, and your partner works Wednesday afternoon to Friday.
- You both work 20 hours per week and you arrange your own schedules.

Call Job Share today at 1-800-JOB-1234

We'll find the right job-share partner for you!

5 *PAIRS.* **Look at the photos. Which of these jobs could two people share? Which jobs would be difficult to share?**

Listening

6 *PAIRS.* **Discuss. What problems can there be when two people share a job?**

7 🎧 **Ken and Marcy share a job at a modeling agency. Listen to their conversation. Then answer the questions.**

1. What job do Ken and Marcy share?
2. What is the problem?

8 🎧 **Listen again and check (✓) the tasks that Marcy did.**

✓ answer the phones
___ send faxes
___ do the copying
___ reply to e-mails
___ call the photographer
___ call the new model
___ make a reservation for lunch

Grammar focus

1 **Look at the examples. Write *R* next to the requests (asking people to do things for you). Write *O* next to the offers (saying you will do things for other people).**

1. A: **Can you call** the restaurant, please? R
   B: Yes, of course.
2. A: **Could you do** this copying? ___
   B: Sorry, I'm afraid I can't.
3. A: **Would you like me to arrange** a meeting for you? ___
   B: Yes, please. I'd like to meet here at the office.
4. A: **Should I make** a reservation at Loon's? ___
   B: Yes, for 1:00, please.
5. A: **I'll send** this fax for you. ___
   B: Thanks!

2 **Look at the examples again. Complete the rules in the chart with *can you, could you, I'll, should I,* and *would you like me to.***

Modals for requests and offers: *can you, could you, I'll, should I,* and *would you like me to*
To make a request, ask a question with ________ or ________ + the base form of the verb. To make an offer, ask a question with ________ or ________ + the base form of the verb, or make a statement with ________ + the base form of the verb.
NOTE: *I'll = I will*

Grammar Reference page 148

3 **Complete the conversations with requests or offers. Use the words in parentheses.**

1. A: Would you like me to call **(would/call)** the airline for you?
   B: Yes, please. ________________ **(could/make)** a reservation for me on the 10:00 A.M. flight?
2. A: ________________ **(can/finish)** the report today?
   B: Sure. Then ________________ **(should/leave)** it on your desk?
3. A: ________________ **(will/arrange)** the meeting for you. Is Friday OK?
   B: Yes, fine. And ________________ **(can/send)** an e-mail to Bernie about it?
4. A: ________________ **(would/get)** a taxi for you?
   B: No. Don't worry. I can do that. But ________________ **(can/check)** the fax machine, please? I'm expecting an important fax.

Pronunciation

4 **Listen. Notice the weak pronunciation of *can, could, should,* and *would* and the way these words are linked to the next word.**

Can you call the restaurant, please?

Could you do this copying?

Should I make a reservation?

Would you like me to arrange a meeting?

Can you send these faxes?

Could you answer the phone?

Should I call a taxi?

Would you like me to do the filing?

5 **Listen again and repeat.**

6 *PAIRS.* **Practice the conversations in Exercise 3.**

Speaking

7 *PAIRS.* **Role-play two situations. Take turns making requests and offers. Student A, look at page 140. Student B, look at page 141.**

A: Can you do the filing, please?
B: Yes, of course. I'll do it this afternoon.

Writing

8 **Choose one of these jobs—travel office clerk, reporter for a TV station, restaurant manager, English teacher—or think of another job. Make a To-do list for the job. Look at the sample To-do list for ideas. Write a memo to your "job share partner." Ask him or her to do some things on the list. Offer to do other things on the list. Give reasons.**

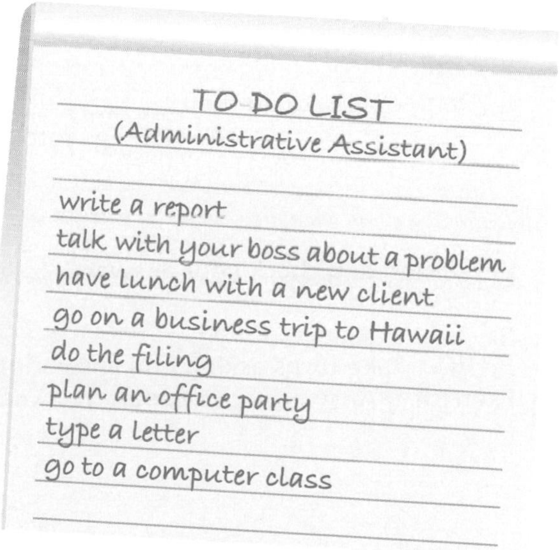
TO DO LIST
(Administrative Assistant)
write a report
talk with your boss about a problem
have lunch with a new client
go on a business trip to Hawaii
do the filing
plan an office party
type a letter
go to a computer class

CONVERSATION TO GO

A: **Could you lend** me some money, please?
B: Sure. And I'll take you to the cash machine on the way home.

UNIT 23

Changing customs

Vocabulary Things you customarily do
Grammar *used to/didn't use to*
Speaking Talking about past customs

Lesson A

Getting started

1 **Complete the questions with the correct words from the box.**

dinner	~~doors~~	food	games	home	horse
housework	long skirts	shoes	slippers		

1. Do men open ___doors___ for women?
2. Do women wear ________________ ?
3. Do families have ________________ together every night?
4. Do women do all the ________________ ?
5. Do people shop for ________________ every day?
6. Do families play ________________ together in the evening?
7. Do people stay ________________ in the evening?
8. Do people travel by ________________ and carriage?
9. Do people take off their ________________ and put on ________________ when they go into a house?

2 **Listen and check your answers.**

3 *PAIRS.* **Take turns asking and answering the questions in Exercise 1. Answer about people you know.**

A ____

B ____

C ____

Reading

4 **Read the article. Then match the paragraphs with the pictures.**

SHOES

Customs and Traditions Around the World

Maybe you don't think about shoes very often. You probably think shoes are boring, but there are very interesting old customs associated with shoes. Here are just a few of them.

D___

E___

1. A long time ago, people used to throw shoes at the bride and groom after the wedding because they thought it was good luck. Some people still tie shoes to the back of the newlywed couple's car.

2. In ancient Rome, a soldier's sandals used to tell everyone how important he was in the army: a captain or a foot soldier.

3. High heels and platform shoes are not new. Hundreds of years ago, people used to wear them in the street because the streets were full of garbage. The garbage didn't touch their feet, so their feet didn't get dirty.

4. In France, when Louis XIV was king, people thought red shoes were very special. Only the very rich aristocracy used to wear them when they visited the king.

5. Strange things happened at Anglo-Saxon weddings. The father of the bride used to give the bride's shoes to the groom. Then the groom used to touch the bride's head with these shoes. This meant that the father no longer owned his daughter—she now belonged to the groom.

5 **Read the article again and write *T* (true) or *F* (false) after each statement.**

1. In some countries, people still throw shoes at the bride at her wedding. F
2. All soldiers in the ancient Roman army wore the same sandals.
3. People wore high heels and platform shoes many years ago.
4. The very rich people wore red shoes when they visited King Louis XIV.
5. At Anglo-Saxon weddings, the groom touched the bride's head with his shoes.

Grammar focus

1 **Study the examples. Notice the difference between the sentences with *used to* and those in the simple past.**

	used to	Simple past
(?)	What **did** they **use to do** at weddings?	What **did** they **do** at your wedding?
(+)	They **used to throw** shoes at the bride and groom.	They **threw** rice at my husband and me.
(–)	Poor people **didn't use to wear** red shoes.	I **didn't wear** red shoes.

2 **Look at the examples again. Circle the correct words to complete the explanations in the chart.**

used to/didn't use to

Use *used to* to talk about something that happened in the past and **still happens / isn't still happening** in the present.

Use *used to* to talk about something that happened **only once / more than once** in the past.

Use the **past form / base form** of the verb after *used to*.

Grammar Reference page 148

3 **Complete the sentences with the correct form of *used to* and a verb from the box.**

~~drink~~	eat	go	open	play	walk	wear

1. In the U.K. one hundred years ago, most people *didn't use to drink* (not) coffee, but now a lot of people do.
2. ____________ men ____________ doors for women in your country fifty years ago?
3. People ____________ (not) in restaurants very often, but now it's more common.
4. When you were a child, ____________ girls ____________ wear jeans to school?
5. One hundred years ago, a young man and woman ____________ (not) for walks without a chaperon.
6. My grandmother ____________ two miles to school every day.
7. ____________ your parents ____________ games with you when you were a child?

Pronunciation

4 **Listen. Notice that *used to* and *use to* are pronounced the same way: "useta."**

used to	Women used to wear long skirts.
didn't use to	Poor people didn't use to wear red shoes.
What did they use to do at weddings?	They used to throw shoes at the bride and groom.

5 **Listen again and repeat.**

Speaking

spending time at home

doing the housework

6 *BEFORE YOU SPEAK.* **Look at the photos. Think about customs and lifestyles 50–100 years ago. Write three sentences about what people used to do. Write three sentences about what people didn't use to do.**

People used to have to go outside to get water.

playing sports

working on the farm

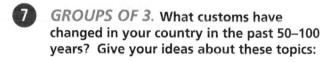

7 *GROUPS OF 3.* **What customs have changed in your country in the past 50–100 years? Give your ideas about these topics:**

- clothes
- food and drink
- communication
- entertainment
- family life
- school
- transportation
- work

In the past, people didn't use to have cars. They used to travel by horse and carriage. Now most people travel by car or motorcycle.

Writing

8 **Write a paragraph about your life when you were a child and your life now. Write about the things you used to do and no longer do—and about things you didn't use to do but you do now. Use *used to/didn't use to.***

CONVERSATION TO GO

A: **Did** women **use to wear** jeans?
B: No. They always **used to wear** skirts or dresses.

UNIT 24

Take a risk

Vocabulary Adventure sports
Grammar Present perfect vs. simple past
Speaking Talking about experiences

Lesson A

Getting started

1 Match the words with the photos.

1. rock climbing A
2. snowboarding ___
3. jet skiing ___
4. parasailing ___
5. snowmobiling ___
6. waterskiing ___
7. scuba diving ___
8. snorkeling ___
9. skateboarding ___
10. windsurfing ___

Pronunciation

2 Listen to the words in Exercise 1. Notice the number of syllables and the stress. Put each word in the correct group.

Oooo	O o o
	rock climbing

3 Listen and check your answers. Then listen again and repeat.

4 *PAIRS.* **Discuss the questions.**

Which sports do you do in the mountains?
Which do you do in the ocean?
Which do you do in the city?
Which of these sports have you tried?

Listening

5 **Listen to the interviews with Andy and Paula, who just arrived at Adventure Zone. Answer these questions.**

1. Which one is on vacation?
2. Why is the other one there?

6 **Listen again to the interview with Andy. Check (✓) each sport he has tried. In the next column, write *Y* if he enjoyed it and *N* if he didn't.**

	Tried it?	Enjoyed it?
snorkeling	✓	
waterskiing		
parasailing		
scuba diving		
windsurfing		

ADVENTURE ZONE

Grammar focus

1 **Study the examples. Notice the difference between the sentences in the present perfect and those in the simple past tense.**

Present perfect	Simple past
(?) **Have** you ever **tried** any dangerous sports?	What sport **did** you **try**?
(+) I**'ve gone** snorkeling.	I **went** snorkeling when I was a kid.
(–) I **haven't gone** windsurfing.	I **didn't go** windsurfing when I was in Puerto Rico.
I**'ve never gone** windsurfing.	

2 **Look at the examples again. Circle the correct words to complete the rules in the chart.**

Present perfect vs. simple past
Use the **simple past / present perfect** to talk about actions that happened at a specific time in the past (yesterday, last Saturday).
Use the **simple past / present perfect** to talk about things that happened at an unspecified time in the past, and when we don't know or it's not important when the action happened.

Grammar Reference page 148

3 **Complete the conversations with the words in parentheses. Use the correct form of the present perfect or simple past.**

1. A: _Have you ever gone_ **(you/ever/go)** parasailing?
   B: No, I ____________________.
2. A: ____________________ **(you/watch)** that program about rock climbing last night?
   B: Yes, I ____________________. It ____________________ **(be)** really interesting.
3. A: ____________________ **(your sister/ever/take)** windsurfing lessons?
   B: No, she ____________________, but she once ____________________ **(try)** waterskiing.
4. A: ____________________ **(you/enjoy)** your adventure vacation last summer?
   B: No, I ____________________. It ____________________ **(be)** terrible.
5. A: I ____________________ **(never/do)** any adventure sports. How about you?
   B: Yes, I ____________________ **(go)** scuba diving for the first time last month.
   A: ____________________ **(you/like)** it?
   B: Yes, I ____________________ **(have)** a wonderful time.

4 ***PAIRS.*** **Practice the conversations in Exercise 3.**

Speaking

5 *BEFORE YOU SPEAK.* **Choose four adventure sports and write four more questions beginning with *Have you ever* . . . .**

Have you ever gone waterskiing?

6 **Interview three students using your questions from Exercise 5. Take notes. Find out . . .**

- who has done these sports.
- who enjoyed/didn't enjoy them.
- who wants to try them.
- who has only watched them.
- what other sports they have done. (Were the sports dangerous?)

7 **Tell the class what you found out about one of your classmates' experience with sports.**

Writing

8 **Write a paragraph to complete your application form for an Adventure Zone vacation.**

ADVENTURE ZONE

APPLICATION

Where the fun never ends!

- **Please tell us about your experience with adventure sports.**
- **Which sports have you done?**
- **Which sports have you not done but want to try?**

CONVERSATION TO GO

A: **Have** you **ever done** any adventure sports?
B: Yes, I **went** snowboarding last week. It was fun!

Review 6 Units 21–24

Unit 21 Long life

1 Listen to the model conversation.

2 Write six statements about things you have done. Use the present perfect tense. Write some true statements, and make up some statements that are not true (but sound possible).

3 *GROUPS OF 3.* Take turns. Say one of your statements aloud. The others in the group say, "True" or "False." A correct guess = 1 point.

Points: ________________

Who is the winner?

Unit 22 Job share

4 Listen to the model conversation.

5 Imagine that you are an administrative assistant in your language school. Make a list of six tasks that you need to do today.

6 *PAIRS.* Role-play. You and your partner share the administrative assistant job. Combine the lists that you wrote in Exercise 5. Take turns. Offer to do some tasks. Ask your partner to do some tasks.

7 Change partners and repeat the role-play.

Unit 23 Changing customs

8 Listen to the model conversation.

9 *PAIRS.* Take turns. Toss a coin (one side of the coin = one point, the other side = two points). Make sentences with a verb from the chart. Use *used to* + the verb to talk about something you used to do as a child, and say how it's different now. Keep score. The person with the most points is the winner.

Verb	_______'s points	_______'s points
be		
go		
have		
watch		
wear		
play		
think about		
TOTAL		

Unit 24 Take a risk

10 Listen to the model conversation.

11 Imagine that you are an extreme athlete. Put a check next to four sports in the second column in the chart. These are the sports you have done.

12 Walk around the room. Find out which sports your classmates have tried. Take turns. Ask *Yes/No* questions. When someone answers, "Yes, I have," write his or her name in the chart. Ask only one question each turn! Try to find one person for each sport.

Adventure sports	Your experience	Find someone who has gone...
1. snowboarding		
2. waterskiing		
3. scuba diving		
4. windsurfing		
5. skateboarding		
6. rock climbing		
7. jet skiing		
8. snowmobiling		

13 *PAIRS.* Compare your answers. Did you find the same people?

UNIT 25

Real fighters

Vocabulary Sports
Grammar *could* and *be good at* for past ability
Speaking Talking about ability in the past

Lesson **A**

Getting started

1 **Complete the chart with the missing words.**

Person (noun)	Sport (noun)	Action (verb)
boxer	boxing	*box*
swimmer		
	running	
skier		
	diving	dive
		skate

2 *PAIRS.* **Discuss the questions.**

Which sports in Exercise 1 do you like to watch? Do you like to do any of these?

Do you know the names of any athletes who do the sports in Exercise 1?

What other athletes do you know? What sports do they do?

Float like a butterfly.
Sting like a bee.
Your hands can't hit
what your eyes can't see.

— Muhammad Ali

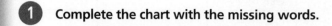

Reading

3 **Look at the photos of the boxers. Guess who they are. What's the connection between them?**

4 **Read the article and check your answers to Exercise 3.**

5 **Read the article again. Write the events from Muhammad Ali's life on the timeline.**

1942	1954	1960
Ali was born		

Laila Ali is Muhammad Ali's daughter. In 1999, at the age of twenty, Laila began boxing. In four years, she won fourteen fights and proved that she could box. But she couldn't beat her father's reputation.

The Greatest

Muhammad Ali was "The Greatest." He was the first boxer to become the heavyweight champion of the world three times. Ali was born in 1942 and was named Cassius Clay. When he was twelve years old, he started boxing. Soon he was really good at boxing. He won the gold medal in boxing at the Olympics in 1960. In 1964, Clay converted to Islam and changed his name to Muhammad Ali.

People noticed more than Ali's boxing—they noticed his personality. He was smart, and he was good at getting media attention. He was famous for saying, "I am the greatest!" He was also a poet, and he could make up poems on any subject: himself, other boxers, and even politics.

As Ali got older, he began to have health problems. He couldn't speak very well or move quickly. In 1984, doctors found that he had Parkinson's disease. Although Ali wasn't able to box anymore, he still had many fans and he could still sign autographs. And he could still help people fight for a better world.

In 1996, the world watched Muhammad Ali light the Olympic torch in Atlanta, Georgia. He couldn't stop the shaking in his hands, but he showed once more that he was "The Greatest."

6 *GROUPS OF 3.* **Read the poem on page 116 by Muhammad Ali. He recited this poem to intimidate other boxers. What does it mean? Discuss.**

1964 — 1984 — 1996

Grammar focus

1 **Study the examples with *could* and *be good at*.**

(+++)	Ali **could**		**really well**.
(++)	They **could**		**well**.
(+)	Laila **could**	**box**	**pretty well**.
(–)	We **couldn't**		**very well**.
(––)	He **couldn't**		**at all**.

(+++)	Ali **was**	**really**		
(++)	They **were**			
(+)	Laila **was**	**pretty**	**good at**	boxing.
(–)	We **weren't**	**very**		sports.
(––)	He **was**	**no**		

2 **Look at the examples again. Circle the correct words to complete the rules in the chart.**

Could **and** ***be good at*** **for past ability**
Could/couldn't is followed by **a noun / the base form of the verb**.
Be good at/not be good at is followed by **a noun / the base form of the verb**.

Grammar Reference page 149

3 **Complete the sentences about past ability with *could* or *be good at*. Use the words in parentheses.**

1. Jane was really good at diving, so she became a diving coach. (really good/diving)
2. Martin ________________, so he joined the school swimming team. (swim/pretty well)
3. I ________________ when I was young, but now I can play pretty well. (no good/playing the piano)
4. They ________________, so they decided to take lessons. (play golf/not very well)
5. We ________________, so we entered the salsa competition. (good/dancing)
6. My brother ________________, so he used to go skiing every weekend. (really good/skiing)
7. She ________________ before she hurt her knee. (run/fast)
8. I ________________, so I didn't enjoy gym class at school. (not very good/sports)
9. He ________________ when he got his first pair of boxing gloves. (box/not at all)

Pronunciation

4 **Listen. Notice the different weak and strong pronunciations of *could*. Notice the strong pronunciation of *couldn't*.**

Could you play the piano?	Yes, I **could**.
How well could you play?	I could play pretty well.
Could you ski?	No, I **couldn't**. I **couldn't** ski at all.

5 **Listen again and repeat.**

Speaking

6 *BEFORE YOU SPEAK.* **Complete the survey about your abilities ten years ago. Add one ability to the list. Use plus (+) and minus (–) signs as in Exercise 1 to show how well you could do each activity.**

PAST ABILITIES SURVEY

Ten years ago, could you . . .	YOU How well?	YOUR PARTNER How well?
swim?		
cook?		
drive?		
play an instrument?		
ride a bike?		
speak a foreign language?		
other? ________________		

7 *PAIRS.* **Interview each other and complete the survey form. Give examples to show how well you could do each activity.**

A: *Could you swim ten years ago?*
B: *Yes, I could. I could swim pretty well.* (Or *I was pretty good at swimming.)*
I could swim a mile without stopping.

8 **Report your partner's answers to the class. Then discuss the results of the survey. Which things could everyone in the class do?**

Writing

9 **Write about a sport or another activity that you could do in the past. Describe the activity and give examples to show how well you could do it. Say whether you can still do it. Use *could* and *be good at*.**

CONVERSATION TO GO

A: **Could** you **drive** when you were in high school?
B: Yes, I **could drive pretty well**, but I **couldn't afford** a car!

UNIT 26

On the go

Vocabulary Travel
Grammar Present perfect: *yet, already*
Speaking Saying what you've done so far

Lesson A

Getting started

1 *PAIRS.* **Look at the picture. Find the words in the box.**

a bag/suitcase	a passport	a pillow	slippers
a teddy bear	a tennis racket	a ticket	a video

2 *PAIRS.* **Look at the picture again. Which things in the picture do you take with you when you travel? Which things do you leave at home? What other things do you take?**

3 **Match the beginnings of the sentences on the left with the correct endings on the right.**

1. Go to the embassy and **apply for** _b_ a. **her passport** soon.

2. She'll have to **renew** ____ b. **a visa** to enter the country.

3. I'm waiting for the bank to **transfer** ___ c. **a car**.

4. Tell the doctor that you need to **get** ___ d. **a hotel** room.

5. I'll fold the clothes, but you **pack** ____ e. **the money**.

6. I'll call the travel agency and **book** ____ f. **online** to buy my tickets.

7. I sometimes call the airline directly, but most of the time I **go**____ g. **a vaccination** against cholera.

 h. **the bags**.

8. We plan to drive around the country so we're going to **rent** ____

Listening

4 🎧 **Melissa is getting ready to go on a trip. Listen to her conversation with a friend. Circle *a* or *b* to answer the questions.**

1. When is Melissa going to travel?
 a. next week b. the week after next
2. Where is she going?
 a. to Cairo b. to Quito
3. What is she going to do there?
 a. relax b. work

5 🎧 **Listen again. Look at the list and check (✓) the travel preparations Melissa has completed.**

TO-DO LIST
- sell the car ✓
- transfer the money
- get my vaccinations
- renew my passport
- apply for a visa
- buy an airline ticket
- make a hotel reservation
- pack my bags

Grammar focus

1 **Study the examples of the present perfect with *yet* and *already*.**

(?) **Have** you **sold** the car **yet**? Yes, I **have**. / No, **not yet**.
(+) I've **already made** a reservation.
(–) She **hasn't called** back **yet**.

2 **Look at the examples again. Complete the rules in the chart with *yet, not yet*, or *already*.**

Present perfect: *yet, already*
Use the present perfect + ________ when an action is complete.
Use the present perfect + ________ when an action is not complete, but we think it will happen.
Use the present perfect + ________ to ask if an action is complete.

Grammar Reference page 149

3 **Complete the phone conversation with *already* or *yet*.**

Mom: Hi, Melissa. Have you finished packing for your trip **(1)** ___yet___?
Melissa: No, not **(2)** ________. But I've gotten my visa **(3)** ________.
Mom: Good. Have you sent me your new email address **(4)** ______?
Melissa: Yes, Mom. And I've **(5)** ________ sent you my new phone number at work.
Mom: Great. Have you called your grandfather **(6)** _____ to say goodbye?
Melissa: No, I haven't called him **(7)** ______. But I've **(8)** ________ called Aunt Rose.
Mom: OK. I've **(9)** ________ emailed my boss that I'll need to take the afternoon off to take you to the airport. He hasn't said OK **(10)** ______, but I'm sure he will.

Pronunciation

4 **Listen. Notice the contracted forms of *have* and *has*.**

I've already sold the car.	She**'s** already sold the car.
I've called my aunt.	She**'s** called her aunt.
I've gotten a visa.	She**'s** gotten a visa.
I've changed my email address.	She**'s** changed her email address.

5 **Listen again and repeat.**

6 *PAIRS.* **Look at Melissa's list on page 121. Take turns making statements about the things Melissa has done. Use contracted forms.**

Speaking

7 *GROUPS OF 3.* **You all work for Matrix International. You're going on a business trip to Spain. Decide who are Students A, B, and C. Look at your To-Do list. Work alone. Check (✓) two things that you've already done.**

Student A TO DO	Student B TO DO	Student C TO DO
- arrange meetings in Spain	- make the hotel reservations	- buy a guidebook
- get the visas	- rent a car	- get travel insurance
- change some money	- get an international driver's license	- tell co-workers about the trip
- book a taxi to the airport	- go online to buy the airline tickets	- make dinner reservations for the first night

8 *GROUPS OF 3.* **Take turns. Ask each other** ***Yes/No*** **questions about the things on the list in Exercise 7. Check (✓) the completed activities. Write notes about when your partners will do the other ones.**

A: Have you made the hotel reservations yet?
B: Yes, I have. OR *No, not yet. I'll do it tomorrow.*

9 **Report to the class about some of the things your group has and hasn't done.**

John hasn't made the hotel reservations yet, but he's going to make them on Friday.

Writing

10 **Think of an important goal you have, such as graduating from school or living in another country. Write about things you have already done to reach your goal and things you haven't done yet.**

CONVERSATION TO GO

A: **Have** you **bought** the tickets **yet**?
B: No, I **haven't done** that **yet**, but **I've already done** everything else!

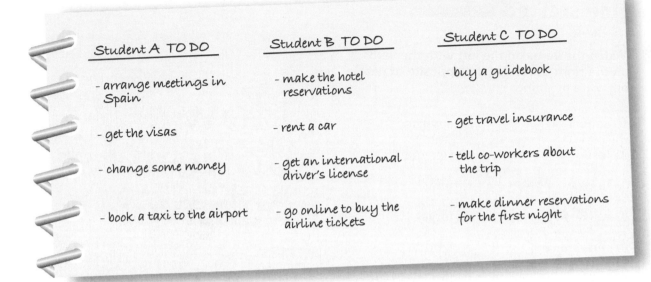

UNIT 27

Behave yourself

Vocabulary Verbs and their opposites
Grammar Present real conditional (*If* + simple present + simple present)
Speaking Talking about consequences

Lesson A

Getting started

1 **Match the verbs on the left with the verbs on the right that have the opposite or nearly opposite meaning.**

1. cancel _b_	a. agree to
2. lose ____	b. schedule
3. borrow ____	c. pull
4. refuse to ____	d. forget
5. remember____	e. lend
6. push ____	f. find

2 **Complete each sentence with a verb from Exercise 1.**

1. I'm going to use the stairs. I _refuse to_ wait any longer for the elevator.
2. Can I __________ your pen, please?
3. You have to __________ the door away from you to close it.
4. Did he __________ his keys again?
5. I'm really pleased that they always __________ my birthday.
6. I'm sorry, but I have to __________ our meeting today.

3 *PAIRS.* **Compare your answers in Exercises 1 and 2.**

How do you behave?

1 **If you forget a friend's birthday, do you:**

A send a card right away and say the mail is slow?
B send a card and apologize for forgetting?
C send no card and say it got lost in the mail?

Reading

4 **Do you have good manners? Take the quiz. Then check the answers in the key below.**

5 *PAIRS.* **Read the quiz again and guess your partner's answers. Compare your answers with your partner's answers. Who has better manners?**

2 If someone pushes a shopping cart in front of you in the supermarket, do you:

A give the person an angry look but say nothing?
B ask the person to please stop?
C push the cart back at the person?

3 If a friend gives you a gift you really don't like, do you:

A take it but never use it?
B take it but use it only when your friend is there?
C take it but give it to someone else?

4 If a friend borrows money from you and forgets to pay you back, do you:

A tell your friend that you need some money and hope he or she remembers?
B ask your friend for the money?
C refuse to talk to your friend until you get the money?

5 A friend cancels a night out with you, saying she has to work. If you see the friend later that evening at the movie theater, do you:

A say nothing?
B ask your friend why she isn't at work?
C refuse to go out with your friend again?

KEY
Mainly A answers: You behave quite well but you aren't always honest. Mainly B answers: You behave very well. Mainly C answers: You don't behave very well at all. Try harder!

Pronunciation

6 **Listen. Notice the different vowel sounds for /ɪ/ in *give*, and /ɛ/ in *forget*.**

/ɪ/	give	gift	if	it
/ɛ/	forget	friend	remember	never

I give ~~h~~im a gift — If I remember, I give ~~h~~im a gift.

I send it later. — If I forget, I send it later.

I never give it away. — If I get a gift from a friend, I never give it away.

7 **Listen again and repeat.**

Grammar focus

1 **Study the examples of the present real conditional.**

If clause	Result clause
(+) **If** I **forget** a friend's birthday,	I **send** a card later.
(–) **If** I **don't remember** a friend's birthday,	I **don't send** a card.
(?) **If** you **forget** a friend's birthday,	**do** you **say** you are sorry?

2 **Look at the examples again. Circle the correct letters to complete the chart.**

Present real conditional

The action in the result clause __________ the action in the *if* clause.

a. depends on   b. doesn't depend on

Use the simple present in ______________.

a. the *if* clause   b. the result clause   c. both clauses

NOTE: Use a comma after the *if* clause when the *if* clause comes first.

Grammar Reference page 149

3 **Complete the present real conditional sentences with the correct forms of the verbs in parentheses.**

1. If he __forgets__ (**forget**) his wife's birthday, he __buys__ (**buy**) her flowers the next day.
2. If my sister __________ (**borrow**) my car, I __________ (**take**) the bus to work.
3. If the weather __________ (**be**) bad, they __________ (**not go**) away for the weekend.
4. If someone __________ (**speak**) very loudly on the train, I __________ (**get**) angry.
5. If he __________ (**not/come**) home at 10:00, his mother __________ (**call**) his friends.
6. If I __________ (**not/have**) enough money, I __________ (**borrow**) some from my friends.
7. If his friends __________ (**ask**) him, __________ (**he/lend**) them his car?

Speaking

4 *PAIRS.* **Think about situations that happen while people are shopping, at a restaurant, at home, or with friends. Write three questions. Begin each one with *If . . . ?* and give three choices in the result clause.**

1 **If** The waiter or waitress brings you the wrong food, **do you:**
A. say nothing but feel angry?
B. remind the waiter or waitress what you ordered?
C. refuse to eat anything?

2 **If** ____________________, **do you:**
A. ____________________?
B. ____________________?
C. ____________________?

3 **If** ____________________, **do you:**
A. ____________________?
B. ____________________?
C. ____________________?

4 **If** ____________________, **do you:**
A. ____________________?
B. ____________________?
C. ____________________?

5 *GROUPS OF 4.* **Take turns asking and answering the questions in your quiz. Do your classmates have good manners?**

Writing

6 **Choose a situation from the quiz on pages 124–125 or from your own quiz above. Write a paragraph describing what you do if you are in that situation. Also explain why you behave that way. Use the present real conditional.**

CONVERSATION TO GO

A: What **do** you **do if** your boss **asks** you to work late?
B: **If** I **want** to keep my job, I **stay** to finish the work!

UNIT 28

Just the job for you

Vocabulary Job descriptions
Grammar *like* + verb + *-ing*, *would like* + infinitive
Speaking Talking about jobs and career preferences

Lesson A

Getting started

1 *PAIRS.* **Look at the photos. Use these phrases to make two sentences describing each job.**

- be active
- be creative
- earn a good salary
- have a lot of responsibility
- travel a lot
- work alone
- work inside
- work outdoors
- work with animals
- work with his/her hands
- work with people
- work with technology

A: A farmer works outdoors.
B: A farmer also works with animals.

Pronunciation

2 **Listen. Notice the /ɚ/ sound.**

work earn learn computer perfect researcher

3 **Listen again and repeat.**

4 **Now listen to these phrases. Notice that /ɚ/ sounds different from the other vowel + *r* in each phrase.**

work outdoors earn more computer software the perfect career market researcher

5 **Listen again and repeat.**

Reading

6 **Read the want ads and match them with the jobs in the photos.**

Do you like creating new menus?
Would you like to join a new catering company?
We cater weddings, parties, and conventions.

Ⓐ chef

Do you like talking to people?
Would you like a flexible schedule?
Would you like to work from home?
We need people to conduct surveys about products for an advertising agency.

Ⓑ ____________

Do you like learning new skills?
Would you like to work with cars and trucks?
Our auto repair business uses state-of-the-art technology.

Ⓒ ____________

Do you like working with technology?
Help people learn to use our new computer software program.

Ⓓ ____________

7 **Read the want ads again and choose:**

- a job you want to do
- a job you don't want to do

8 *GROUPS OF 3.* **Discuss your answers to Exercise 7. Explain the reasons for your choices.**

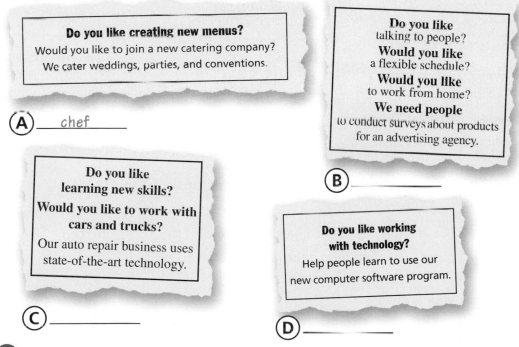

Grammar focus

1 **Study the examples. Notice the difference between the sentences with *like* and those with *would like.***

like + verb + *-ing*	*would like* + infinitive
(?) **Do** you **like working** with people? (Yes, I **do**. / No, I **don't**.)	**Would** you **like to work** from home? (Yes, I **would**. / No, I **wouldn't**.)
(+) I **like learning** new skills.	I**'d like to be** a mechanic.
(–) I **don't like working** outside.	I **wouldn't like to be** a chef.

2 **Look at the examples again. Circle the correct words to complete the rules in the chart.**

like, would like
Use *like* + verb + *-ing* to talk about **a future possibility / present likes and dislikes**.
Use *would like* + infinitive to talk about **a future possibility / present likes and dislikes**.

Grammar Reference page 149

3 **Complete the conversation with *(not) like* or *would (not) like*.**

A: I **(1)** *'d like* to get a new job.

B: What **(2)** ________ you ________ to do in your next job?

A: Well, I love computers, and I **(3)** ________ working with technology. I'm not really a "people person," so I don't think I **(4)** ________ to work with people all the time.

B: OK, how about computer repair? **(5)** ________ you ________ to learn how to fix computers?

A: That sounds interesting. I've never tried it, but I **(6)** ________ to fix things, I think.

B: OK, are you interested in fixing cars?

A: No, I **(7)** ________ to be an auto mechanic. I hate getting dirty. I **(8)** ________ to try computer repair. I think that might be just the job for me!

4 **Listen and check your answers.**

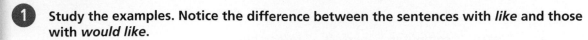

Speaking

5 *BEFORE YOU SPEAK.* **Write down three jobs you would like to do and three jobs you would not like to do. Write them on a piece of paper. Keep this list for later.**

6 **Look at the questionnaire for choosing a job. Add 3 more questions.**

Choosing a Job Questionnaire

Do you like working with people?
Would you like to travel?
Do you want to work outdoors?

7 *PAIRS.* **Take turns asking and answering your questions from Exercise 6.**

8 **Write down three jobs you think your partner would like to do and three jobs you think your partner would *not* like to do.**

Jobs my partner would like:
1.
2.
3.

Jobs he or she wouldn't like:
1.
2.
3.

9 *PAIRS.* **Take turns comparing your lists from Exercises 5 and 8. Explain why you chose each job for yourself and for your partner.**

I think you'd like to work as a mechanic. I chose that job for you because you like working with your hands and you like being active.

Writing

10 **Think of a job you would like to have. Write a want ad for that job. Use the want ads on page 129 as a model.**

Conversation to Go

A: **Do** you **like working** here?
B: No, I **don't**.
A: **Would** you **like to work** abroad?
B: Yes, I **would**.

Review 7 Units 25–28

Unit 25 Real fighters

1 Look at the picture and listen to the model conversation.

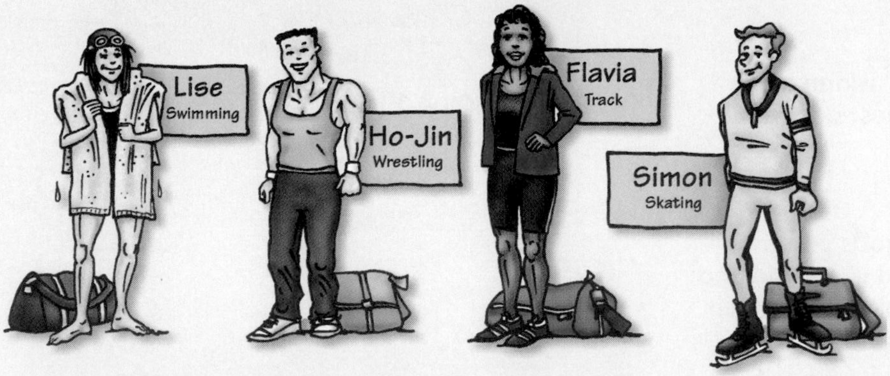

2 *PAIRS.* The people in the pictures are athletes. Find out how well they could do sports ten years ago. Student A, look at page 138. Student B, look at page 141.

3 Compare your charts. Are they the same? Who is the best athlete?

Unit 26 On the go

4 Look at the picture and listen to the model conversation.

5 *GROUPS OF 4.* Rafael is going on a trip. Look at the picture and the To-do list. You have one minute. Remember all the things Rafael has and hasn't done to prepare for his trip.

Close your book. Write sentences about what Rafael has and hasn't done. You have 5 minutes. The group with the most sentences wins.

Points: ____________________

Rafael has booked a hotel. He hasn't gotten a haircut yet.

Unit 27 Behave yourself

6 *GROUPS OF 4.* Look at the situations. Think of problems that may happen for each situation. Complete the chart.

Situation	Problem
1. You lend your friend $100.	
2. It's your friend's birthday.	
3. You borrow your friend's bicycle.	
4. Your friend gives you a gift.	
5. You and your friend have a date to go to dinner.	

7 🎧 Listen to the model conversation.

8 *GROUPS OF 4.* Discuss each situation. Agree on the best thing to do for each.

9 Report back to the class. Choose a situation. What is the best thing to do?

Unit 28 Just the job for you

10 🎧 Look at the job profiles and listen to the model conversation.

Name: Mark
What would you like to do?
- work with children
- be active
- work outside
Is there anything you don't like?
- doing a lot of paperwork
Jobs: Coach

Name: Sun-Ju
What would you like to do?
- work with my hands
- work alone
- be creative
Is there anything you don't like?
- working from 9 to 5 every day
Jobs: ____________

Name: Bruno
What would you like to do?
- work with technology
- earn a good salary
- work inside
Is there anything you don't like?
- traveling a lot
Jobs: ____________

11 *PAIRS.* Look at the job profiles again and discuss what each person would like to do in his or her next job. Think of two jobs that each person could do.

12 Report to the class. What's the best job for each person? Explain why you chose it.

World of Music 4

This Used to Be My Playground

Madonna

Vocabulary

1 **Match the expressions with their meanings.**

Expression

1. Don't look back. c
2. Keep your head held high. ___
3. This was my childhood dream. ___
4. Don't hold onto the past. ___
5. Life is short. ___
6. No regrets. ___
7. This is our pride and joy. ___
8. My heart is breaking. ___

Meaning

a. Be proud of yourself.
b. I wanted this when I was very young.
c. Don't think about the past.
d. I'm very sad.
e. We're very proud of this.
f. Live in the present.
g. Use your time carefully, because you won't live forever.
h. Don't feel bad about past events.

2 **The title of the song is "This Used to Be My Playground." What is a playground? What do you think the song will be about?**

The 90s

In the 1990s, ***Madonna*** *became not just a pop superstar but a movie star as well.* "This Used to Be My Playground" *is from one of her movies,* A League of Their Own.

Listening

3 **Listen to the song. Circle *a* or *b* to answer the questions.**

1. What is the singer thinking about?
   a. She's remembering the past.
   b. She's thinking about the future.
2. Who is she talking to in the song?
   a. someone she met a long time ago
   b. someone she met recently

4 **Listen to the song again. Complete the lyrics on page 135 with the words you hear.**

5 *PAIRS.* **Compare your answers in Exercise 4.**

This Used to Be My Playground

[Chorus]
This used to be my playground.
This used to be my childhood ____________.
This used to be the place I ____________ to.
Whenever I was in need of a ____________.
Why did it have to end?
And why do they always say:

Don't look ____________.
Keep your ____________ held high.
Don't ask them why,
Because ____________ is short.
And before you know,
You're feeling old,
And your ____________ is breaking.
Don't hold on to the ____________.
Well, that's too much to ask.

[Chorus]

No regrets,
But I ____________ that you were
here with me.
Well then there's ____________ yet.

I can see your ____________
in our secret ____________.
You're not just a memory.
Say good-bye to yesterday
Those are words I'll ____________.

This used to be my ____________.
This used to be our pride and joy.
This used to be the place we ran to
That no one in the ____________
could dare destroy.

This used to be our playground. (used to be)
This used to be our childhood dream.
This used to be the place we ran to.
I wish you ____________ here with me.

This used to be my playground. (Ah, ah, ah)
This used to be my childhood dream.
This used to be the place we ran to.
The best things in life are always ____________.
Wishing you ____________ here with me.

Speaking

6 *GROUPS OF 3.* **Discuss these questions.**

1. What feeling do you get from this song? Why do the music and words make you feel that way?
2. Look at some expressions from the song. Do you think these expressions give good advice? Why or why not?
   a. Don't look back.
   b. Keep your head held high.
   c. Life is short.
   d. No regrets.

Unit 2, Exercise 6
Student A

Make these phone calls to Student B. Apologize and make an excuse.

I'm afraid I can't come to work. I have a terrible headache.

1. You have a headache, and you can't go to work. Call your boss.
2. You want to watch a baseball game tonight, but your friend wants you to go to a movie with him/her. Call your friend, Student B, and make an excuse for not going to the movies.
3. Your boss wants you to go out for dinner with a client, but you have a dentist appointment at 6:00. Call your boss, Student B.

Answer these phone calls from Student B. Listen to his/her problems. Show sympathy.

That's too bad.

4. You're an English teacher. Student B is your student.
5. You're a manager in an office. Student B is an employee in your department.
6. You're going to move into your new apartment tomorrow. Student B is your friend.

Review 1, Exercise 10
Student A

Dario is going on a trip. Take turns asking questions to fill in his schedule.

Where is he going to go on Saturday? What's he going to do on Sunday?

Dario's Travel Schedule 8 days/7 nights

Day	Where	What
Sat.	fly into the city	visit a museum
Sun.	drive down the coast	
Mon.		
Tues.		attend a festival
Wed.	drive to the mountains	
Thurs.		
Fri.		buy souvenirs at a market
Sat.		~~X~~

Unit 6, Exercise 8

Read the email messages and write replies to each one.

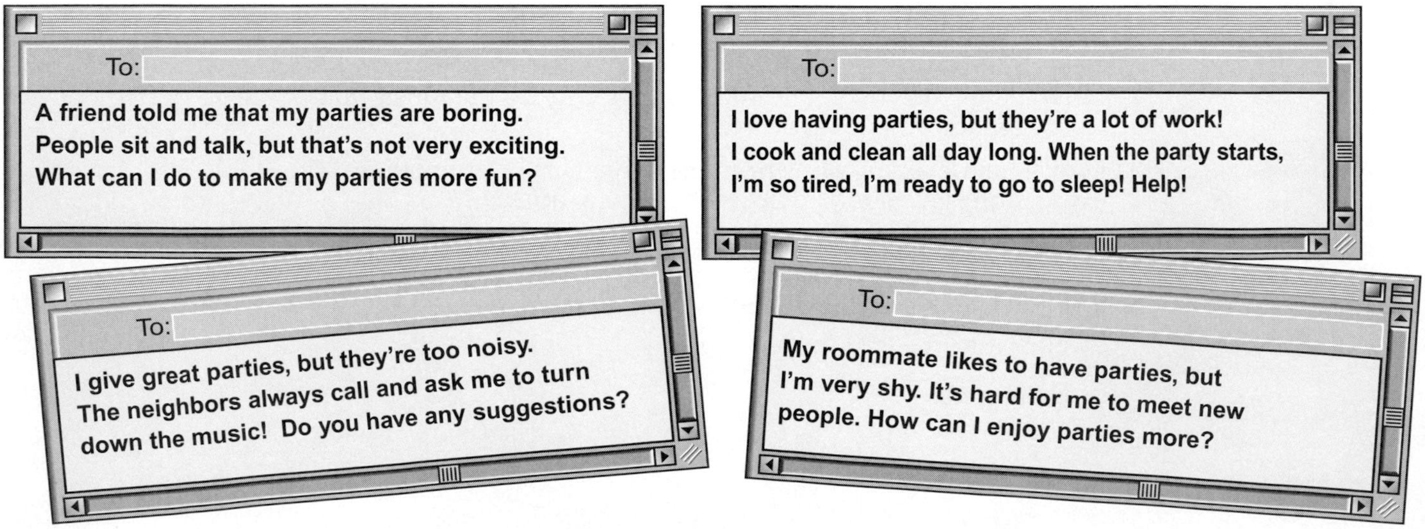

To:
A friend told me that my parties are boring. People sit and talk, but that's not very exciting. What can I do to make my parties more fun?
To:
I love having parties, but they're a lot of work! I cook and clean all day long. When the party starts, I'm so tired, I'm ready to go to sleep! Help!
To:
I give great parties, but they're too noisy. The neighbors always call and ask me to turn down the music! Do you have any suggestions?
To:
My roommate likes to have parties, but I'm very shy. It's hard for me to meet new people. How can I enjoy parties more?

Unit 7, Exercise 6
Student A

Student A, begin. Look at these pictures of your colleagues from another office. Give each person a name. Then describe each one to your partner. Your partner will show you the person in the picture on page 33. Is your partner correct?

A: My colleague, Sandra Vazquez, is going to arrive on Saturday. Can you meet her at the airport?

B: Sure. What does she look like?

A: She . . .

Now, switch roles. Look at page 33.

Review 2, Exercise 8
Student A

Student A, begin. Describe the person in your picture A. Then Student B will describe the person in his or her picture A. Is it the same person? Then Student B continues with picture B.

Picture A   Picture B   Picture C   Picture D

Unit 2, Exercise 6
Student B

Answer these phone calls from Student A. Listen to his/her problems. Show sympathy.

That's too bad.

1. You're a supervisor. Student A is your employee.
2. You want to go to the movies tonight. Student A is your friend.
3. You're a supervisor. Student A is your employee.

Make these phone calls to Student A. Apologize and make an excuse.

I'm sorry, but I can't come to class today. I have a fever.

4. You can't go to your English class because you have a fever. Call your teacher, Student A.
5. You have a sore throat and cough. There's an important meeting at work. Call your boss, Student A, and apologize for not going to the meeting.
6. Your friend, Student A, wants you to help him move into a new apartment, but you don't want to. Call your friend and make an excuse.

Review 1, Exercise 10
Student B

Dario is going on a trip. Take turns asking questions to fill in his schedule.

What's he going to do Saturday? Where is he going to go on Sunday?

Dario's Travel Schedule 8 days/7 nights

Day	Where	What
Sat.	fly into the city	visit a museum
Sun.		go swimming
Mon.	go on safari	
Tues.		
Wed.		go hiking
Thurs.	take a bus to the lake	
Fri.		buy souvenirs at a market
Sat.	fly home	

Review 7, Exercise 2
Student A

Look at the chart. Ask questions to find out how well each athlete could do sports ten years ago. (Don't look at your partner's chart.)

Athlete	Sport	10 years ago
Lise 		–
		– –
		+
Ho-Jin 		

Flavia 		+ +
		+
		– –
Simon 		

Symbol	Meaning	
+++	could . . . really well	be really good at . . .
++	could . . . well	be good at . . .
+	could . . . pretty well	be pretty good at . . .
–	couldn't . . . very well	be not very good at . . .
– –	couldn't . . . at all	be no good at . . .

Unit 7, Exercise 6
Student B

Student B, look at these pictures of your colleagues from another office. Give each person a name. Then describe each one to your partner. Your partner will show you the person in the picture on page 33. Is your partner correct?

B: *My colleague, Carlos Lopez, is going to arrive on Saturday. Can you meet him at the airport?*
A: *Sure. What does he look like?*
B: *He...*

Review 2, Exercise 8
Student B

Student A will describe the person in his or her picture A. Then you will describe the person in your picture A. Is it the same person? Then continue with picture B.

Picture A

Picture B

Picture C

Picture D

Unit 6, Exercise 6

Look at the costs in the worksheet. Put a check (✓) next to your suggestions.

Party Planning Worksheet

		Cost	Check (✓)
Location	At school/home/the office	$0	
	Hotel	$150	
Food and beverages	Snacks (chips, cheese, sandwiches, soft drinks)	$75	
	Buffet dinner with soft drinks	$150	
	Formal dinner with soft drinks and wine	$275	
	Dessert buffet	$100	
	Ice cream	$50	
	Cookies	$30	
Music	Band	$150	
	DJ	$75	
	CD player	$0	
Entertainment	Photographer	$75	
	Games	$100	
	Celebrity guest	$300	
	Total:		

Review 4, Exercise 13
Student A

Student A, you're at the supermarket. Call Student B to ask what you should buy.

Switch roles. Student A, look at the food in the picture. Tell Student B what food you have at home and suggest what he or she needs to buy.

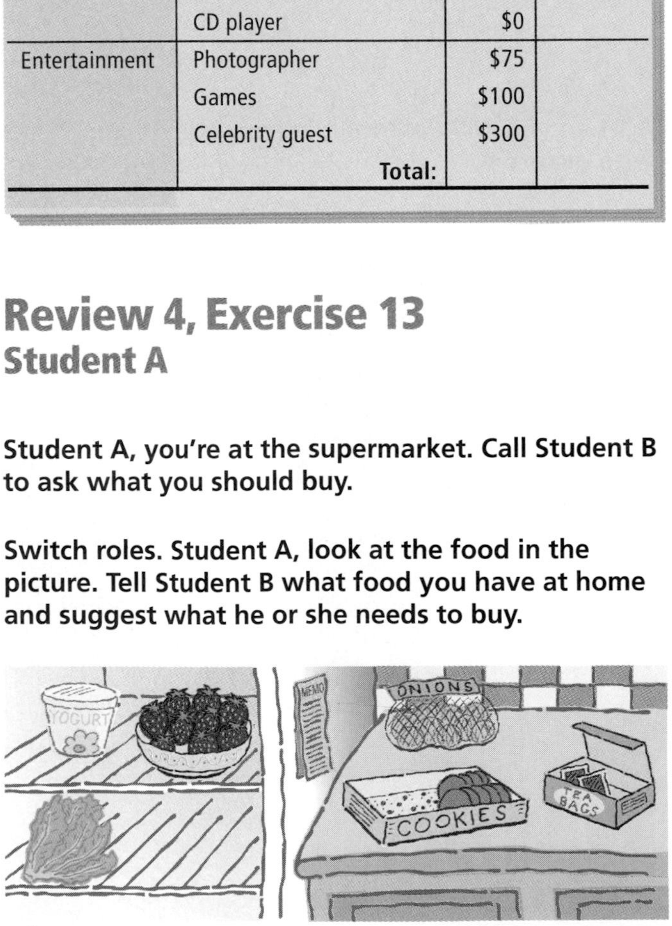

Unit 18, Exercise 7

There were 16 people in the picture on page 85. Try to answer these questions about each person:

- What were they doing?
- What were they wearing?
- Where were they in the picture?

A man was chasing his dog. He was wearing a red jacket.

Unit 22, Exercise 7
Student A

Use the phrases to make your requests and offers.

Requests	Offers
Can you...?	Would you like me to...?
Could you...?	Should I...?
	I'll...

A: Can you do the filing, please?
B: Yes, of course. I'll do it this afternoon.

- **Situation 1**
  You're an executive at a television station. Student B is your assistant. Ask Student B to:
  a. send a fax.
  b. make a dinner reservation at the Lemon Tree Restaurant.
  c. type a letter.

- **Situation 2**
  You're a shoe salesperson in a department store. Student B is the store manager.
  a. You're waiting on a customer. Your boss asks you to do something. Offer to do the task after you finish with the customer.
  b. You hurt your back on the weekend. You think Bob (another salesperson) can help. Offer to ask Bob.
  c. You're going to the sandwich shop for lunch. Your boss asks you to do something. Offer to do the task after lunch.

Review 7, Exercise 2
Student B

Look at the chart. Ask questions to find out how well each athlete could do sports ten years ago. (Don't look at your partner's chart.)

Athlete	Sport	10 years ago
Lise 		

Ho-Jin 		+ +
		+
		–
Flavia 		

Simon 		+ +
		+
		–

Symbol	Meaning	
+++	could . . . really well	be really good at . . .
++	could . . . well	be good at . . .
+	could . . . pretty well	be pretty good at . . .
–	couldn't . . . very well	be not very good at . . .
– –	couldn't . . . at all	be no good at . . .

Unit 22, Exercise 7
Student B

Use the phrases to make your requests and offers.

Requests	Offers
Can you . . .?	Would you like me to . . .?
Could you . . .?	Should I . . .?
	I'll . . .

A: Can you do the filing, please?
B: Yes, of course. I'll do it this afternoon.

- **Situation 1**
  You're an administrative assistant at a television station. Student A is your boss. Use this information when your boss makes a request:
  a. The fax machine is broken. Offer to send an email instead.
  b. The Lemon Tree Restaurant is closed. Offer to try some other restaurants.
  c. You're busy typing a report. Your boss asks you to do something. Offer to do the task after you finish the report.

- **Situation 2**
  You're the manager of a department store. Student A is a salesperson in the shoe department. Ask Student A to:
  a. put the shoes back in the storeroom.
  b. help you move a large box.
  c. put *Sale* signs on certain shoe racks.

Unit 9, Exercise 7
Students B and C

You are customers at Rosie's Restaurant. Look at the menu. Decide what you would like and give your order to your waiter/waitress.

Waiter: Would you like to order?
Customer: Yes. I'd like the chicken in herb sauce.

Rosie's Restaurant

Appetizers	Cup	Bowl
Tomato soup	$3.25	$4.00
Chicken soup	$3.25	$4.00
Soup of the day	$3.25	$4.00

Entrées	
Pasta with tomato sauce	$8.95
Pasta with garlic sauce	$9.95
Chicken in herb sauce	$12.95
Shrimp with vegetables	$15.95

Side dishes	
French fries	$2.25
Garden salad	$2.95
Mixed vegetables	$2.75
Rice	$2.25

Desserts	
Ice cream *Chocolate or vanilla*	$3.00
Cake	$4.25
Cheesecake	$5.00

Review 4, Exercise 13
Student B

Student B, look at the food in the picture. Tell Student A what food you have at home and suggest what he or she needs to buy.

Switch roles. Student B, you're at the supermarket. Call Student A to ask what you should buy. Write a shopping list.

Review 1, Exercise 10
Student C

Dario is going on a trip. Take turns asking questions to fill in his schedule.

Where is he going to go on Sunday? What is he going to do on Saturday?

Dario's Travel Schedule 8 days/7 nights

Day	Where	What
Sat.	fly into the city	
Sun.		
Mon.		see elephants and lions
Tues.	visit the countryside	
Wed.		
Thurs.		do water sports
Fri.	return to the city	
Sat.		

Unit 1

Simple present and adverbs of frequency

- Use ***how often*** to ask about frequency.
  __How often__ do you go to the movies?
  __How often__ does Mary visit you?
- Use adverbs of frequency (***never, sometimes, usually, often, always***) with the present tense to say how often something happens.
  Do they __always__ go out on Saturday?
  She __usually__ goes to a café.
  Peter doesn't __often__ watch TV.
  We __sometimes__ get takeout.
  I __never__ work late.

Notes:

- Adverbs of frequency go after the verb ***be***, but before all other verbs.
  It__'s always__ noisy.
  John __often runs__ after work.
- The adverb ***sometimes*** can also go at the beginning of a sentence.
  __Sometimes__ we get takeout.

Unit 2

Linking words: *and, but, so*

- Use the words ***and***, ***but***, and ***so*** to connect ideas.
- Use ***and*** to connect similar ideas.
  I have a headache, __and__ my stomach hurts. (I have two problems.)
- Use ***but*** to connect different ideas.
  I have a headache, __but__ my stomach feels okay. (I only have one problem: a headache.)
- Use ***so*** to show a result.
  I took some aspirin, __so__ I feel better. (I feel better because I took aspirin.)

Unit 3

Simple past: regular and irregular verbs

- Use the simple past to talk about completed actions in the past, often with a specific time reference (*in 1990, yesterday, last year*, etc.).
- Add **–d** or **–ed** to regular verbs to form the simple past in affirmative statements.
  A television station __hired__ her.
  She __wanted__ to be famous.
- Some verbs are irregular in the simple past. (See the list on page 150.)
  She __got__ a job in television.
  People __began__ to notice her.

Negative	Subject + ***didn't*** + base form of the verb *She __didn't finish__ college.* *Her parents __didn't have__ a lot of money.*
Question	**Did** + subject + base form of the verb ***Did*** *people* ***like*** *her television program?* ***Did*** *she* ***make*** *movies?*
Short answers	**Yes** + subject + ***did*** **Yes**, *she* ***did***.
	No + subject + ***didn't*** **No**, *she* ***didn't***.

Unit 4

Be going to for future

- Use ***be going to*** to talk about future plans.

Affirmative	Subject + ***be going to*** + base form of the verb *I__'m going to see__ the Rocky Mountains.* *It__'s going to be__ crowded there.*
Negative	Subject + ***be*** + ***not*** + ***going to*** + base form of the verb *You__'re not going to travel__ with me.* *I__'m not going to take__ a lot of stuff.*
Question	***Be*** + subject + ***going to*** + base form of the verb ***Is*** *the weather* ***going to be*** *sunny?* ***Are*** *the markets* ***going to be*** *open?*
Short answers	***Yes*** + subject + ***be*** ***Yes****, it* ***is****.*
	No + subject + ***be*** + ***not*** ***No****, it* ***isn't****.*

Notes:

- The form of ***be*** must agree with the subject.
  __I am going to__ travel.
  __You aren't going to__ snorkel.
  __She's going to__ speak English.
  __We're going to__ go on a safari.
  __They're going to__ sightsee.
- You can use the present continuous ***going to*** instead of ***going to go*** to talk about traveling.
  __We're going to go__ to India.
  __We're going to__ India.

Unit 5

Modals: *should* and *shouldn't* for advice

- Use ***should*** to give and ask for advice.

Affirmative	Subject + ***should*** + base form of the verb *You **should** shake hands.* *She **should** take a gift.*
Negative	Subject + ***shouldn't*** + base form of the verb *We **shouldn't** take our shoes off.* *They **shouldn't** arrive late.*
Question	***Should*** + subject + base form of the verb ***Should** we shake hands?* ***Should** she use first names?*
Short answers	***Yes*** + subject + ***should*** ***Yes**, you **should**.*
	No + subject + ***shouldn't*** ***No**, she **shouldn't**.*

Unit 6

Expressions for making suggestions

Use ***why don't, let's (not), maybe . . . could,*** and ***how about*** to make suggestions.

- ***Why don't*** + subject + base form of the verb
  *Why **don't** we have a party?*
  *Why **don't** you come?*
- ***Let's (not)*** + base form of the verb
  ***Let's** take something.*
  ***Let's not** make salad.*
- ***Maybe*** + subject + ***could***
  ***Maybe** you **could** take drinks.*
  ***Maybe** he **could** get ice.*
- ***How about*** + verb + *–ing*
  ***How about** playing some games?*
  ***How about** listening to some music?*

Unit 7

Be and *have* with physical descriptions

- Use ***be*** to talk about people's ages.
  ***I'm** 34. How old **are** you?*
- Use ***be*** to talk about people's height.
  *You **are** short, and he **is** average height.*
- Use ***be*** to talk about people's weight.
  *She **is** slim, but her sisters **are** heavy.*
- Use ***have*** to talk about people's eyes.
  *Ben and Jeff **have** green eyes, but Ann **has** blue eyes.*
- Use ***have*** to talk about people's hair.
  *She **has** long hair, but he **has** short hair.*
- Use ***have*** to talk about people's facial hair.
  *Keith **has** a mustache, but he **doesn't have** a beard.*

Exception: Use ***be*** with ***bald***.
*Ken has thick hair, but his father **is** bald.*

Unit 8

Say and *tell*

- ***Say*** and ***tell*** are irregular verbs in the simple past.
  *say → **said*** *tell → **told***
- Always use an object pronoun (***me, you, him, her, it, us, them***) or a noun with ***told***.
  *I **told you** that I saw the movie.*
  *You **told me** that you didn't like it.*
  *He told **John** about making movies.*
- Never use an object pronoun or noun with ***said***.
  *She **said** that she loved* Dr. No.
  *We **said** that Halle Berry was a great actress.*
- Use the present after ***say*** or ***tell*** and the past after ***said*** or ***told***.
  She ***says*** *that* Casablanca *is a good movie.*
  *She **said** that she **liked** black-and-white films.*
  *He **tells** me that* Star Wars ***is*** *his favorite movie.*
  *He **told** me that he **loved** the special effects.*

Note: You don't have to use the word ***that*** with ***say*** or ***tell***.
She said she liked black-and-white films.
He told me he loved the special effects.

Unit 9

Would like/like, would prefer/prefer

- Use ***like*** and ***prefer*** to talk about the things you usually like.
  *I **like** shrimp.*
  *He **likes** going out to dinner.*
  *We **prefer** red wine to white.*
  *She **prefers** small restaurants to large ones.*
- Use ***would like*** and ***would prefer*** to talk about the things that you want at this moment or in the future.
  ***Would** you like a drink?*
  ***I'd** like a glass of water, please.*
  ***Would** you prefer the chicken or the shrimp?*
  *We**'d prefer** the chicken tonight, thanks.*

Notes:
- Use the contraction ***'d*** for ***would*** in affirmative sentences.
  *I**'d like** the fish.*
  *We**'d prefer** red wine.*
- Use ***prefer*** to show a choice between two things.
  *I **prefer** juice to soda.*

Unit 10

Will for predicting

- Use ***will*** and ***will not (won't)*** to make predictions about the future.

Affirmative	Subject + ***will ('ll)*** + base form of the verb *People **will** travel more.* *We**'ll** take vacations to the moon.*
Negative	Subject + ***will not (won't)*** + base form of the verb *People **won't** use cars as much.* *We **won't** pollute the environment.*
Question	***Will*** + subject + base form of the verb ***Will** types of transportation change?* ***Will** the population of the world increase?*
Short answers	***Yes*** + subject + ***will*** ***Yes**, it **will**.*
	No + subject + ***won't*** ***No**, it **won't**.*

- Also use ***I think*** and ***I don't think*** with ***will/won't*** to make predictions about the future.
  *I think we**'ll** use the Internet more.*
  *I think people **won't** write letters anymore.*
  *I don't think there **will** be hotels in space.*
  *Do you think we**'ll** fly private jets instead of driving cars?*

Note: When using ***I think*** with ***will/won't***, be careful to form negatives and short answers correctly. (***Think*** is in the present.)

*I don't think **I'll** go.*
X I think I won't go.

*Do you think **we'll** survive?*
Yes, I do.
X Yes, I will.

Unit 11

Have to/don't have to

- Use ***have to*** to say that something is necessary.
  *I **have to** get up early to go to work.* (It's necessary.)
  *I **don't have to** get up early on Sundays.* (It's not necessary.)
  ***Do** you **have to** use a computer at work?*

Affirmative	Subject + ***have/has to*** + base form of the verb *I **have to** work a lot.* *She **has to** travel for her job.*
Negative	Subject + ***don't/doesn't have to*** + base form of the verb *Doctors **don't have to** sell things.* *The salesperson **doesn't have to** type.*
Question	***Do/Does*** + subject ***have to*** + base form of the verb ***Do** you **have to** work on weekends?* ***Does** your boss **have to** review your work?*
Short answers	***Yes*** + subject + ***do/does*** ***Yes**, she **does**.*
	No + subject + ***don't/doesn't*** ***No**, she **doesn't**.*

Note: Use ***do/does*** (not ***have/has***) in short answers.

Do you have to work late?
*Yes, I **do**.*
X Yes, I have.
*No, I **don't**.*
X No, I haven't.

Unit 12

Present perfect for indefinite past: *ever, never*

- Use the present perfect to talk about events that happened at an unspecified time in the past.

Affirmative	Subject + ***have/has*** + past participle *I **have traveled** a lot.* *He **has spent** time outdoors.*
Negative	Subject + ***haven't/hasn't*** + past participle *We **haven't worked** on a farm.* *She **hasn't grown** food.*
Question	***Have/has*** + subject + past participle ***Have** you **lived** overseas?* ***Has** it **rained** a lot?*
Short answers	***Yes*** + subject + ***have/has*** ***Yes**, I **have**.* ***Yes**, it **has**.*
	No + subject + ***haven't/hasn't*** ***No**, I **haven't**.* ***No**, it **hasn't**.*

- Use ***ever*** to make a question with the present perfect.
  *Have you **ever** traveled overseas?*
- Use ***not*** or ***never*** to make a negative statement with the present perfect.
  *No, I have**n't**. I have **never** traveled overseas.*

Note: To form the past participle of regular verbs, add ***–d*** or ***–ed*** to the base form of the verb. There is a list of irregular verbs on page 150.

Unit 13

Review: possessive *'s*

- Use ***'s*** after people's names or singular nouns to show possession.
  *They're the family**'s** photos.*
  *It's not Lisa**'s** jewelry box.*
  *Where is James**'s** watch?*
- Use **'** after regular plural nouns to show possession.
  *That is my grandparents**'** trunk.*
  *The boys**'** photos are in the album.*
- Use ***'s*** after irregular plural nouns.
  *The children**'s** toys are upstairs.*
  *Where are the women**'s** dresses?*

Possessive adjectives

- Use possessive adjectives (***my, your, his, her, its, our, their***) to replace a possessive noun in a sentence.
  *This is Paul's guitar. → This is **his** guitar.*
  *That is the dog's bed. → That is **its** bed.*

Note: it's = it is; its = possessive adjective

Possessive pronouns

- Use possessive pronouns (***mine, yours, his, hers, ours, theirs***) to replace a possessive adjective and the noun it describes.
  *They're my books. → They're **mine**.*
  *It's our house. → It's **ours**.*

Belong to

- Use the verb ***belong to*** to talk about things that a person has or owns.
  *The book **belongs to** me.* (I own the book.)
  *The dolls **belong to** Cindy.* (Cindy owns the dolls.)

Unit 14

Adverbs of manner; comparative adverbs

- Use adverbs of manner to tell how an action is done.
  *You asked **rudely**, but I answered **politely**.*
- Many adverbs of manner are formed by adding ***–ly*** to an adjective.
  *proud → proud**ly***
  *polite → polite**ly***
  *kind → kind**ly***
  *suspicious → suspicious**ly***
- Use ***more/less*** + adverb of manner + ***than*** to compare two actions.
  *Mapela talks **more quickly than** Haneko.*
  *Haneko talks **more slowly than** Mapela.*

Notes:

- For adjectives ending in ***–y***, change the ***y*** to ***i***, then add ***–ly***.
  happy → happ**ily**
  angry → angr**ily**
- **Well** is the adverb form of **good**.
  *Mahala is a **good** singer.*
  *Mahala sings **well**.*

Unit 15

Verbs for *likes/dislikes* + noun/verb + *–ing*

- Use a noun or the base form of a verb + ***–ing*** after ***like***, ***love***, and ***hate***.
  *I **like** jogging.*
  *You **love** jogging, but you **hate** swimming.*
  *We **don't like** aerobics.*
  ***Do** they **like** sports?*
  *Yes, he **loves** playing tennis, and she **loves** golf.*

Unit 16

Quantifiers: *some, any, much, many, a lot of*

For count and non-count nouns

- Use ***some*** in affirmative statement when you don't know the exact quantity or if quantity isn't important.
  *I have **some** bread.*
  *She bought **some** apples.*
- Use ***any*** in negative statements and questions.
  *He didn't get **any** cheese.*
  *Did we buy **any** oranges?*
- Use ***a lot of*** in affirmative and negative statements and questions to talk about a large quantity.
  *Do you eat **a lot of** fresh fruit?*
  *We eat **a lot of** fresh fruit.*
  *I don't eat **a lot of** fruit, but I eat **a lot of** vegetables.*
  *She eats **a lot of** apples.*

For count nouns

- Use ***many*** in negative statements and questions.
  *I don't eat **many** vegetables.*
  *How **many** tomatoes are there?*
  *Are there **many** apples?*

For non-count nouns

- Use ***much*** in negative statements and questions.
  *I don't spend **much** money.*
  *How **much** milk is there?*
  *Is there **much** yogurt?*

Unit 17

Modals: *have to/had* to for present and past necessity

Present

- Use ***have to*** to say that something is necessary.
  *I **have to** go to work today.* (Work is required. I don't have a choice.)
  *I **don't have to** go to work today.* (Work isn't required. It is Sunday, and the office is closed.)

Past

- Use ***had to*** to say that something was necessary in the past.
  *I **had to go** to work yesterday.* (Work was required. I didn't have a choice.)
  *I **didn't have to** go to work today.* (Work wasn't required. It was a holiday, and the office was closed.)

Unit 18

Simple past and past continuous

- Use the past continuous to talk about a past action that was happening over a period of time.
  *The police **were working** all night.*
- Use the simple past to talk about a completed past action.
  *A witness **saw** the crime.*
- Use the simple past and past continuous together in one sentence if the first action was still going on when the second action happened.
  *The man **was running away** when the police **arrived**.*
  (First, the man started running away. He was still running away. Then the police arrived.)
  *I **was reading** when I **heard** a noise.*
  (First, I started reading. I was still reading. Then I heard a noise.)

Unit 19

Because, for, and infinitives of purpose

- Use the words ***because***, ***for***, or an infinitive verb to answer the questions *why* and *what for*.
- Use ***because*** followed by a clause to talk about purpose.
  *I went to the bank **because** I needed money.*
  *She bought a sandwich **because** she was hungry.*
- Use ***for*** followed by a noun to talk about purpose.
  *I went to the bank **for** a new checkbook.*
  *She bought a sandwich **for** a snack.*
- Use an infinitive verb (sometimes followed by a noun) to talk about purpose.
  *I went to the bank **to get** some money.*
  *She bought a sandwich **to eat**.*

Unit 20

Indefinite and definite articles: *a/an, the*

- Use ***a/an*** the first time you talk about something.
  A *young couple has* ***an*** *old house.*
- Use ***the*** to talk about the same thing again.
  The *couple turns* ***the*** *house into a hotel.*
- Use ***the*** when there is only one example of something.
  The *moon goes around* ***the*** *Earth.*
- Use ***the*** with superlative adjectives.
  The Mousetrap *is* ***the*** *most famous murder mystery.*
- Use ***the*** to talk about something specific.
  I don't like ***the*** *ice cream at that restaurant.*
  Did you enjoy ***the*** *music at the show?*
- Don't use ***the*** to talk about things in general.
  I like ice cream. It's my favorite dessert.
  X I like the ice cream.

Unit 21

Present perfect: *how long/for/since*

- Use the present perfect to talk about actions or states that started in the past and continue into the present.
  I've lived *here for a long time.* (I came here a long time ago, and I still live here.)
  We've known *each other since 1992.* (We met in 1992, and we still know each other.)
- Use ***how long*** with the present perfect to ask about length of time.
  How long *have you had your dog?*
  How long *has she studied French?*
- Use ***for*** to talk about length of time.
  I've had him ***for*** *two years.*
  She has studied it ***for*** *four months.*
- Use ***since*** to say when the action started.
  I've had him ***since*** *last March.*
  She has studied it ***since*** *January.*

Unit 22

Modals: requests and offers

- Use ***will*** in affirmative statements to offer to do things for people.
  I'll *send the faxes for you.*
  I'll *help you after lunch.*
- Use ***should*** and ***would you like me to*** in questions to offer to do things for people.
  Should *I send the faxes for you?*
  Would you like me to *help you after lunch?*
- Use ***can*** and ***could*** to ask people to do things for you.
  Can *you photocopy this, please?*
  Could *you answer the phone?*

Unit 23

Used to/didn't use to

- Use ***used to*** followed by the base form of the verb to talk about things that generally happened in the past, but that don't happen now.

Affirmative	Subject + ***used to*** + base form of the verb *I* ***used to*** *drink a lot of coffee* (but now I don't).
Negative	Subject + ***didn't use to*** + base form of the verb *Women* ***didn't use to*** *wear pants in public* (but now they do).
Question	***Did*** + subject ***use to*** + base form of the verb ***Did*** *families* ***use to*** *spend more time together?*
Short answers	***Yes*** + subject + ***did*** ***Yes****, they* ***did****.*
	No + subject + ***didn't*** ***No****, they* ***didn't****.*

Unit 24

Present perfect vs. simple past

- Use the present perfect (***have/has*** + past participle) to talk about events up to now. It isn't important when the events happened.
  I've gone *rock climbing with my friends.*
  (refers to some time in the past; it doesn't matter when)
  Have *you* ***ever been*** *to Switzerland?*
  (refers to any point in the past)
  Sophie ***has never gone snorkeling****.*
  (refers to all time in the past)
- Use the simple past to talk about completed actions in the past, often with a time reference.
  I ***went*** *rock climbing a lot when I* ***was*** *younger.*
  (refers to a past action; I don't go anymore)
  Did *you* ***go*** *to Switzerland?*
  (refers to a specific time or trip in the past)
  Sophie ***didn't go snorkeling*** *when we were in Cancun.*
  (refers to a specific time or trip in the past)

Unit 25

Could and be good at for past ability

- Use ***could/couldn't*** to talk about abilities in the past.

Affirmative	Subject + ***could*** + base form of the verb *He* ***could*** *hit a baseball really far.* *We* ***could*** *ski fast.*
Negative	Subject + ***couldn't*** + base form of the verb *They* ***couldn't*** *run very quickly.* *I* ***couldn't*** *dive.*
Question	***Could*** + subject + base form of the verb ***Could*** *you wrestle when you were younger?* ***Could*** *she win competitions?*
Short answers	***Yes*** + subject + ***could*** ***Yes****, she* ***could****.*
	No + subject + ***couldn't*** ***No****, she* ***couldn't****.*

- Also use ***be/not be good at*** + a noun to talk about abilities in the past.
  Ali ***was good at*** *boxing.*
  The swimmer ***wasn't good at*** *skiing.*
  Were *you* ***good at*** *sports?*
- Use adverbs of degree to (***really***, ***pretty***, ***very well***, ***at all***) emphasize past abilities.

He	***could*** swim ***really well***. **was really good at** swimming.
She	***could*** swim ***pretty well***. ***was pretty good at*** swimming.
We	***couldn't*** swim ***very well***. ***weren't very good at*** swimming.
You	***couldn't*** swim ***at all***. ***were no good at*** swimming.

Unit 26

Present perfect: *yet, already*

- Use ***already*** with the present perfect when the action is completed. (It is not important when it happened.)
  I've ***already*** *received the visas in the mail. (Here they are.)*
  She's ***already*** *packed her bags.* (The bags are ready.)
- Use ***not yet*** when the action is not completed but you think that it will happen.
  I haven't found my passport ***yet****.* (But I will.)
  We haven't rented a car ***yet****.* (We don't have one now, but we will get one.)
- Use ***yet*** to ask if an action is complete.
  Has she left ***yet****?* (Is she still there or did she leave?)
  Have you called your sister ***yet****?* (Do you still need to call or did you finish calling?)

Unit 27

Present real conditional (*If* + simple present + simple present)

- Use the present real conditional to talk about things that are usually true.
  If *I* ***forget*** *a friend's birthday, I say I'm sorry.*
  If *I* ***need*** *a ride to work, my dad drives me.*
  If *she* ***doesn't have*** *money, I lend it to her.*
  Does *he get angry* ***if*** *she forgets their anniversary?*

Note: The ***if*** clause can go before or after the main clause. Use a comma to separate the two clauses *only* when the ***if*** clause comes first.

If *it rains, I take the bus.*
I take the bus ***if*** *it rains.*

Unit 28

Like **+ verb + *–ing, would like* + infinitive**

- Use **like** + verb + ***–ing*** to talk about your present likes and dislikes.
  I ***like*** *learning new skills.*
  I ***don't like*** *working outside.*
  Do *you* ***like*** *helping people?*
- Use ***would like to*** + the base form of the verb to imagine future possibilities.
  I'd like *to be a teacher.*
  I ***wouldn't like*** *to be a farmer.*
  Would *you* ***like*** *to write books?*

Irregular Verbs

Simple present	Simple past	Past participle
be	was/were	been
become	became	become
begin	began	begun
break	broke	broken
build	built	built
buy	bought	bought
catch	caught	caught
choose	chose	chose
come	came	come
cost	cost	cost
do	did	done
draw	drew	drawn
drink	drank	drunk
drive	drove	driven
eat	ate	eaten
fall	fell	fallen
feel	felt	felt
fight	fought	fought
find	found	found
fly	flew	flown
forget	forgot	forgotten
get	got	gotten
give	gave	given
go	went	gone
grow	grew	grown
hang	hung	hung
have	had	had
hear	heard	heard
hurt	hurt	hurt
keep	kept	kept
know	knew	known
leave	left	left
lend	lent	lent
lose	lost	lost
make	made	made
mean	meant	meant
meet	met	met
pay	paid	paid
put	put	put
quit	quit	quit

Simple present	Simple past	Past participle
ride	rode	ridden
read	read	read
run	ran	run
say	said	said
see	saw	seen
sell	sold	sold
send	sent	sent
shake	shook	shaken
show	showed	shown
sing	sang	sung
sit	sat	sat
sleep	slept	slept
speak	spoke	spoken
spend	spent	spent
stand	stood	stood
swim	swam	swum
take	took	taken
teach	taught	taught
tell	told	told
think	thought	thought
throw	threw	thrown
understand	understood	understood
wear	wore	worn
win	won	won
write	wrote	written

Unit 1
get takeout
go for a walk
go out for dinner
go to the beach
go to the gym
go to the movies
meet friends
rent a video
sleep late
stay home
watch TV
work late

Unit 2
arm
back
ear
eye
foot
hand
head
leg
mouth
nose
stomach
throat
a cold
a cough
a fever
a headache
a sore throat
a stomachache
I hurt my . . . .
My . . . is/are sore.

Unit 3
be born
find a job
get married
give money to charity
go to school
graduate from school
grow up
have children
work hard

Unit 4
Australia
Africa
Asia
Canada
England
Europe
India
Ireland
Italy
Korea
North America
South Africa
coast
countryside
market
monuments
mountains
safari

Unit 5
arrive on time
bow
exchange business cards
give a gift
kiss
shake hands
take a flowers
take your shoes off
use first names/last names
visit someone's home
wear a suit

Unit 6
a birthday party
a costume party
a going-away party
afford
buy
cost
pay
rent
spend

Unit 7
age
elderly
middle-aged
young
height
average height
short
tall
weight
average weight
heavy
slim
hair
black
blond
brown
curly
dark
bald
beard
long
mustache/moustache
sideburns
straight

Unit 8
action movie
comedy
science fiction movie
romantic film
actress
actor
director
special effects
scenery
amazing
black-and-white film
classic
excellent
exciting
fantastic
fast
good
interesting
slow

Unit 9
customer
waiter
menu
appetizer
entree
side dish
cappuccino
coffee
espresso
tea
dessert

cheesecake
chocolate ice cream
raspberry sorbet
fork
glass
knife
napkin
pepper
salt
spoon
garden salad
herbs
mixed vegetables
olives
pasta
rice
sauce
shrimp
soup of the day
tomatoes

Unit 10
climate
communication
economy
government
politics
population
prediction
space
technology
transportation

Unit 11
arrange meetings
communicate
give presentations
make decisions
make money
meet with clients
travel
type letters and contracts
wait on customers
work as a team
work long hours

Unit 12
build a house
catch a fish
cook for a group
grow food
have an adventure
make clothes
spend time
start a business
take care of animals
teach a class
travel abroad
use a computer
work on a farm
write an article

Unit 13
ballet shoes
baseball glove
camera
doll
jewelry box
photo album
pin
shawl
toy truck
watch
fall apart
fall out
give away
pass on
put away
throw away
take out
try on

Unit 14
absent-minded
ashamed
bad-mannered
calm
embarrassed
forgetful
loud
polite
proud
relaxed
rude
suspicious
trusting
upset

Unit 15
aerobics
baseball
basketball
biking
golf
hockey
jogging
karate
skiing
soccer
swimming
tennis
volleyball

Unit 16
bread
chocolate
cookies
fruit
juice
lettuce
onions
oranges
salt
strawberries
vegetables
water
yogurt

Unit 17
break
casual
commute
downsize
flextime
formal
full-time
part-time
supervisor
telecommute

Unit 18
police officer
intruder
suspect
victim
witness

confess
get arrested
investigate
question
report

Unit 19
clothing store
coffee house
convenience store
drugstore
hair salon
newsstand
restaurant
blouse
blow-dry
bottle of aspirin
candy bar
cup of coffee/tea
haircut
magazine
perfume
sandwiches
shampoo
socks
T-shirt

Unit 20
actors
applaud
audience
chairs
composer
costumes
musical
performers
play
playwright
opera
scenery
seats
spectators
theater

Unit 21
a couple of days/weeks/months/years
a long time
ages
more than five days/weeks/months/years
noon
New Year's Eve
over ten days/weeks/months/years
the day before yesterday
two days/weeks/months/years ago

Unit 22
arrange a meeting
do the copying
file the notes
get an email
have an appointment
leave a message
make a reservation
send a fax
sign your name

Unit 23
do housework
have dinner
open doors
play games
put on your slippers
shop for food
stay home
take off your shoes
travel by horse and carriage
wear skirts

Unit 24
jet skiing
parasailing
rock climbing
scuba diving
skateboarding
snorkeling
snowboarding
snow mobiling
waterskiing
windsurfing

Unit 25
boxer/boxing/box
diver/diving/dive
runner/running/run
skater/skating/skate
skier/skiing/ski
swimmer/swimming/swim
wrestler/wrestling/wrestle

Unit 26
a pillow
slippers
a teddy bear
a tennis racket
a ticket
a video
apply for a passport
book a hotel room
get a vaccination
go online
pack a bag
renew a visa
rent a car
transfer money

Unit 27
agree to
borrow
cancel
find
forget
lend
lose
pull
push
refuse to
remember
schedule

Unit 28
be active
be creative
conduct surveys
earn a good salary
have a lot of responsibility
help people learn
travel a lot
work alone
work inside
work outdoors
work with animals
work with his/her hands
work with people
work with technology

Acknowledgments

The authors and series editor wish to acknowledge with gratitude the following reviewers, consultants, and piloters for their thoughtful contributions to the development of *WorldView*.

BRAZIL: São Paulo: Sérgio Gabriel, **FMU/Cultura Inglesa, Jundiaí;** Heloísa Helena Medeiros Ramos, **Kiddy and Teen;** Zaina Nunes, Márcia Mathias Pinto, Angelita Goulvea Quevedo, **Pontifícia Universidade Católica;** Rosa Laquimia Souza, **FMU-FIAM;** Élcio Camilo Alves de Souza, Marie Adele Ryan, **Associação Alumni;** Maria Antonieta Gagliardi, **Centro Britânico;** Chris Ritchie, Debora Schisler, Sandra Natalini, **Sevenidiomas;** Joacyr Oliveira, **FMU;** Maria Thereza Garrelhas Gentil, **Colégio Mackenzie;** Carlos Renato Lopes, **Uni-Santana;** Yara M. Bannwart Rago, **Associação Escola Graduada de São Paulo;** Jacqueline Zilberman, **Instituto King's Cross;** Vera Lúcia Cardoso Berk, **Talkative Idioms Center;** Ana Paula Hoepers, **Instituto Winners;** Carlos C.S. de Celis, Daniel Martins Neto, **CEL-LEP;** Maria Carmen Castellani, **União Cultural Brasil Estados Unidos;** Kátia Martins P. de Moraes Leme, **Colégio Pueri Domus;** Luciene Martins Farias, **Aliança Brasil Estados Unidos;** Neide Aparecida Silva, **Cultura Inglesa;** Áurea Shinto, **Santos:** Maria Lúcia Bastos, **Instituto Four Seasons. CANADA:** Stella Waterman, **Camosun College. COLOMBIA: Bogota:** Sergio Monguí, Rafael Díaz Morales, **Universidad de la Salle;** Yecid Ortega Páez, Yojanna Ruiz G., **Universidad Javeriana;** Merry García Metzger, **Universidad Minuto de Dios;** Maria Caterina Barbosa, **Coninglés;** Nelson Martínez R., **Asesorías Académicas;** Eduardo Martínez, Stella Lozano Vega, **Universidad Santo Tomás de Aquino;** Kenneth McIntyre, **ABC English Institute. JAPAN: Tokyo:** Peter Bellars, **Obirin University;** Michael Kenning, **Takushoku University;** Martin Meldrum, **Takushoku University;** Carol Ann Moritz, **New International School;** Mary Sandkamp, **Musashi Sakai;** Dan Thompson, **Yachiyo Chiba-ken/American Language Institute;** Carol Vaughn, **Kanto Kokusai High School. Osaka:** Lance Burrows, **Osaka Prefecture Settsu High School;** Bonnie Carpenter, **Mukogawa Joshi Daigaku/ Hannan Daigaku;** Josh Glaser, Richard Roy, **Human International University/Osaka Jogakuin Junior College;** Gregg Kennerly, **Osaka YMCA;** Ted Ostis, **Otemon University;** Chris Page, **ECC Language Institute;** Leon Pinsky, **Kwansei Gakuin University;** Chris Ruddenklau, **Kinki University;** John Smith, **Osaka International University. Saitama:** Marie Cosgrove, **Surugadai University. Kobe:** Donna Fujimoto, **Kobe University of Commerce. KOREA: Seoul:** Adrienne Edwards-Daugherty, Min Hee Kang, James Kirkmeyer, Paula Reynolds, Warren Weappa, Matthew Williams, **YBM ELS Shinchon;** Brian Cook, Jack Scott, Russell Tandy, **Hanseoung College. MEXICO: Mexico City:** Alberto Hern, **Instituto Anglo Americano de Idiomas;** Eugenia Carbonell, **Universidad Interamericana;** Cecilia Rey Gutiérrez, María del Rosario Escalada Ruiz, **Universidad Motolinia;** Salvador Castañeda, Alan Bond, Eduardo Fernández, Carla Silva, **Universidad Panamericana;** Raquel Márquez Colin, **Universidad St. John's;** Francisco Castillo, Carlos René Malacara Ramos, **CELE – UNAM/Mascarones;** Belem Saint Martin, **Preparatoria ISEC;** María Guadalupe Aguirre Hernández, **Comunidad Educativa Montessori;** Isel Vargas Ruelas, Patricia Contreras, **Centro Universitario Oparin;** Gabriela Juárez Hernández, Arturo Vergara Esteban Juan, **English Fast Center;** Jesús Armando Martínez Salgado, **Preparatoria Leon Tolstoi;** Regina Peña Martínez, **Centro Escolar Anahuac;** Guadalupe Buenrostro, **Colegio Partenon;** Rosendo Rivera Sánchez, **Colegio Anglo Español;** María Rosario Hernández Reyes, **Escuela Preparatoria Monte Albán;** Fernanda Cruzado, **Instituto Tecnológico del Sur;** Janet Harris M., **Colegio Anglo Español;** Rosalba Pérez Contreras, **Centro Lingüístico Empresarial. Ecatepec:** Diana Patricia Ordaz García, **Comunidad Educativa Montessori;** Leticia Ricart P., **Colegio Holandés;** Samuel Hernández B., **Instituto Cultural Renacimiento. Tlalpan:** Ana María Cortés, **Centro Educativo José P. Cacho. San Luis Potosí:** Sigi Orta Hernández, María de Guadalupe Barrientos J., **Instituto Hispano Inglés;** Antonieta Raya Z., **Instituto Potosino;** Gloria Carpizo, **Seminario Mayor Arquidiocesano de San Luis Potosí;** Susana Prieto Noyola, Silvia Yolanda Ortiz Romo, **Universidad Politécnica de San Luis Potosí;** Rosa Arrendondo Flores, **Instituto Potosino/Universidad Champagnat;** María Cristina Carmillo, María Carmen García Leos, **Departamento Universitario de Inglés, UASLP;** María Gloria Candia Castro, **Universidad Tecnológica SLP;** Bertha Guadalupe Garza Treviño, **Centro de Idiomas, UASLP. Guadalajara:** Nancy Patricia Gómez Ley, **Escuela Técnica Palmares;** Gabriela Michel Vázquez, Jim Nixon, **Colegio Cervantes Costa Rica;** Abraham Barbosa Martínez, Lucía Huerta Cervantes, Paulina Cervantes Fernández, Audrey Lizaola López, **Colegio Enrique de Osso;** Ana Cristina Plascencia Haro, Joaquín Limón Ramos, **Centro Educativo Tlaquepaque III;** Rocío de Miguel, **Colegio La Paz;** Hilda Delgado Parga, **Colegio D'Monaco;** Claudia Rodríguez, **English Key. León:** Laura Montes de la Serna, **Colegio Británico A.C.;** Antoinette Marie Hernández, **"The Place 4U2 Learn" Language School;** Delia Zavala Torres, Verónica Medellín Urbina, **EPCA Sur;** María Eugenia Gutiérrez Mena, Ana Paulina Suárez Cervantes, **Universidad la Salle;** Herlinda Rodríguez Hernández, **Instituto Mundo Verde;** María Rosario Torres Neri, **Instituto Jassa. Aguascalientes:** María Teresa Robles Cázares, **Escuela de la Ciudad de Aguascalientes / Universidad de Aguascalientes;** María Dolores Jiménez Chávez, **ECA – Universidad Autónoma de Aguascalientes;** María Aguirre Hernández, **ECA – Proyecto Start;** Fernando Xavier Gómez Orenday, **UAA – IEA "Keep On";** Felisia Guadalupe García Ruiz, **Universidad Tecnológica;** Margarita Zapiain B., **Universidad Autónoma de Aguascalientes;** Martha Ayala Cardoza, **Universidad de la Concordia / Escuela de la Ciudad de Aguascalientes;** Gloria Aguirre Hernández, **Escuela de la Ciudad de Aguascalientes;** Hector Arturo Moreno Díaz, **Universidad Bonaterra.**